Horse Crazy

HORSE CRAZY

WOMEN *and the* HORSES *They* LOVE

Edited by A. BRONWYN LLEWELLYN

Adams Media
Avon, Massachusetts

Published by Adams Media, an F+W Publications Company
57 Littlefield Street
Avon, MA 02322
www.adamsmedia.com
Printed in the United States of America.
ISBN 13: 978-1-59337-453-2
ISBN 10: 1-59337-453-4

J I H G F E D C B

Library of Congress Cataloging-in-Publication Data
Horse crazy / edited by A. Bronwyn Llewellyn.
p. cm.
ISBN 1-59337-453-4
1. Horses—Anecdotes. 2. Horsemen and horsewomen—Anecdotes. 3. Human-animal relationships—Anecdotes. I. Llewellyn, A. Bronwyn (Anita Bronwyn)

SF301.H64 2005
636.1—dc22

2005016009

Interior illustrations by Michelle Dorenkamp.

To Meera, Alyce, Kathryn, Kay, Odette, and Benedicte, old friends and new, for sharing and encouraging my horse craziness

Acknowledgments

It hardly seems proper for the editor to take credit for this anthology when the credit more accurately goes to the staff at Adams Media for entrusting me with their project, particularly Kate Epstein, Bridget Brace, Meredith O'Hayre, and the rest of the editorial staff, without whose guidance and hard work this book would not be what it is.

Very special thanks go to Paula Munier, who no doubt pegged me for this project after spending two days with me watching an amateur dressage competition during a time of upheaval and uncertainty in both our lives. Horses eased us through that transition and I expect they will help us through many more.

Last, but certainly not least, my deepest thanks go to all the wonderful, horse-crazy women captured in these stories and to all who contributed stories that we weren't able to publish here. Their unique experiences, passion for horses, and, at times, wry humor, are what make this collection special.

Contents

INTRODUCTION

A song by Australian singer Kasey Chambers begins, "When I grow up, I want a pony . . ." I still feel that way. Horses have filled my heart from as far back as I can remember. A black-and-white photograph of me at four years old shows a chubby girl in a cowgirl ensemble—hat, fringed vest and skirt, boots, and self-satisfied smile—astride a stick horse with a stuffed vinyl head and tiny reins. When I couldn't have a real horse, I compensated by drawing them—herds of them—probably decimating whole forests of trees in the process.

Beryl Markham, adventurer and the daughter of a racehorse trainer, once wrote, "A lovely horse . . . is an emotional experience of the kind that is spoiled by words." On horseback, with a warm breeze ruffling your hair, words are superfluous. But in recalling that moment, that day, or that special horse, words give life to memory. And words allow the rest of us to participate in each other's unique experiences.

Volumes have been written about the exceptional bond between horse and human. This anthology explores one aspect of that phenomenon: the extraordinary relationship between horse and woman. Mystical, paranormal, otherworldly—whatever you call it—there is no doubt that this bond exists and that it is powerful and even life changing. When you and a horse find your bond, it is a gift like no other: irreplaceable, irrepressible, and inexplicable.

The women and horses in these pages fulfill dreams, overcome physical or emotional obstacles, and heal bones and hearts. Each of these writers knows that horses have contributed to the person she is today—some dramatically, and others in more subtle ways. From the United Kingdom to British Columbia, and North Carolina to California, these writers offer evocative facets of the precious treasure that is the horse-woman bond. The horses in these stories offer something a dog, parakeet, hamster, or any other pet can't (or in the case of cats, won't): friendship, trust, camaraderie, or perhaps most important of all, freedom.

Reading these stories, once again I feel that vicarious thrill of galloping on horseback that I could always find in books or my imagination. This horse-woman bond was something I accepted as fact, but could never confirm with firsthand proof. Here is proof.

—A. BRONWYN LLEWELLYN

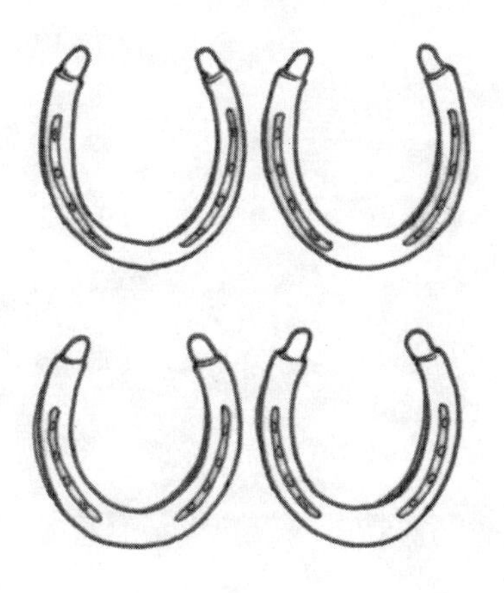

The Gift Horse

Would you be interested in buying my mare?" asked my neighbor.

"No." My previous encounters with female equines had been disastrous, and I wasn't exactly winning all the ribbons with my gelding, either. To soften my terse response, I added, "Give me her details, and I'll ask my friends if they know anyone needing a horse."

"She's an Irish Thoroughbred ex-racehorse," said my neighbor. "Fifteen three, sixteen years old, chestnut, and going cheap because she cribs and windsucks."

Great, I thought, *every horsewoman's dream!* Cribbing and windsucking—gripping any available surface with the teeth then swallowing air—are two vices that reduce a horse's value considerably. They wear down the front teeth, allegedly cause colic, and according to common wisdom, pass the habit to stable mates.

I tried to sound polite. "What's she done?"

"Only trail riding. She's really good in traffic, but she hasn't been ridden for two years."

A must-have horse.

We lived in England at the time. I casually mentioned our neighbor's "desirable" mare to my husband and a visiting friend, Don. "How much does she want?" Don asked. Initially baffled at his question, I remembered he would soon lose his own chestnut mare in a pending divorce.

"Eight hundred pounds, including tack," I answered warily. "Why?"

"Call her up. I'll try the horse tomorrow."

"You *cannot* be serious!" I knew where that horse would live if Don bought her—at our place.

The following morning my husband drove our mad friend to see the horse, Kelly. The horse was hastily being shod while windsucking for England. An hour later, Don rode her into our field, where she promptly bucked him off. When he remounted, I suggested he use our enclosed riding arena. This time he fared better.

That night, our intrepid friend became the owner of a new mare, saddle, bridle, and a saddle blanket, now completely threadbare on both sides. I had never seen an uglier horse. Ribs poked through her worm-ridden belly. Her lower lip protruded, her tongue hung out, muscles bulged in the wrong places from her vices . . . the list was endless. All of us wondered about Kelly's former life.

To curb the cribbing and windsucking in her new home—our stables—we slammed on a crib collar. When tied up, she'd break free and gallop down our drive. If we moved anything on the ground by her feet, the same thing happened. She'd bite when being saddled and when the bit was put in her mouth. When Don tightened her girth before getting on, she'd bite *and* cow-kick for good measure.

Once mounted, Kelly was fairly calm except in front of a fence, where she morphed into an equine dynamo. There was no stopping her. There was also no stopping her from stopping. Don fell off a lot.

But he was very brave and entered her in a cross-country competition. She dumped him at the *trakehner* (a log suspended over a ditch), and then galloped off. She was finally caught and held for Don to remount. As our friend's foot reached the stirrup, Kelly flung herself onto the ground in full view of the crowd.

Don was humiliated. His red witch rose from the dirt, shook herself off, and bolted. *Anyone interested in a cheap chestnut mare?*

Don asked me to sell her for him, and I wasn't happy. I'd have to show that minx to any prospective buyer, which meant actually sitting on her.

Strangely, I felt sorry for the little horse. She had looked so pitiful when she came to us that first winter, with raw blanket rubs around her chest and between her hind legs. We discovered that a tendon injury had banished her to the same field for two years, while her equine companions came and went. She hated her blanket because her former owner had left it on her for months. I imagined the cow-kicking resulted from tightening her girth too much and too quickly. Boredom and frustration had fostered her bad habits.

Knowing all that didn't necessarily give me the courage to ride her. But in order to sell her, I would have to do just that.

I attached her next to a haynet—we don't use cross-ties in England—then groomed her with deep strokes while she munched away. She seemed to enjoy the attention and even dozed. But when I placed the saddle on her back, her ears flattened menacingly. She wasn't asleep anymore! I fed her a distracting tidbit while I buckled the girth very loosely. No kick. I put on her bridle and gave her another treat, which she chewed instead of me. There was also no cow-kick when I offered a last bribe before retightening the girth. Then I mounted her—very slowly. I knew the stunt she'd pull if she didn't like her rider.

I sat mousy quiet, afraid to apply any aids. She stayed calm through the walk, trot, and canter, so I approached a cross-pole and hung onto a tuft of mane as Kelly hurled herself over it.

I wanted to get off, but a buyer would want to see her jump; I had to keep going. "Let the fence come to you," I remembered my instructor telling me. I repeated it over and over as I steered the hurdle racer toward one upright fence, then a wider one. Boy, could she jump! I looked at my husband, and we both thought the same thing: *This is a good horse! Completely nuts—but talented.*

That night, over the phone, Don gave Kelly to me. He was happy she was going to a good home, but I wondered if I was ready for the huge challenge ahead.

I decided not to put any pressure on Kelly—no specific shows, no agenda. This was important since there was much to work on, and I had no pretensions of being a great rider.

When she was annoyed, Kelly would jiggle the bit in her teeth and toss her head. She also chucked her head up at every canter strike off. When she trotted, her head swayed side to side. Without warning, she'd lean on my hands to avoid proper contact. She rushed her fences. Her tongue hung out almost all the time. There was indeed much room for improvement.

I exercised her daily, gradually increasing the length of our flatwork sessions. My instructor helped, without laughing, for which I was grateful. Every time Kelly performed one of her little "things" I'd say, "We don't do that any more," and firmly believed she would stop. I simply pretended she didn't have those endearing quirks, and after several months, they had dwindled to nothing—save the hanging tongue, which defeated me. But the horse moved beautifully, and for the first time in my riding career, I didn't feel like a pathetic amateur.

Finally, it was time for our first dressage show together. It took us over an hour to load her into the trailer. At the show, she stomped and whinnied and scared everyone, including me. During the competition, she whirled violently around the arena. Mercifully, it was indoors so she couldn't escape. The judge gave me the lowest score possible, but kindly commented that I'd "ridden with sensitivity."

The next few months were busy. I exposed Kelly to everything, including show jumping, hunter trials, and combined training. She systematically jumped out of dressage arenas and ditched me at ditches. What she did jump, she steeplechased at a hundred miles an hour. If I forgot her tidbit while I tightened her girth, she kicked me in the thighs. Those were exhilarating times.

So why did I, the most average of average horsewomen, persevere? Because, slowly, something good was happening. At shows, Kelly's anxiety level decreased. She began to trust me and jump the fences she had once refused. As my confidence grew, we became partners.

Kelly proved this one day. Two friends tacked her up for a competition while I walked the course. I returned to find my horse rearing, tossing her head, and preparing to break loose. "She won't let us put on her tendon boots," said my friends.

I patted Kelly's neck and said quietly, "It's Mum." She immediately stopped fretting and let me apply the boots. My friends were no more astounded than I.

Six months after that first dressage debacle, we returned to the same venue and performed the same test. This time, Kelly moved like a hot knife through butter *and* kept her tongue in her mouth. We had to leave before the final results were announced, but I left behind an envelope for the ribbon I was sure we had earned.

That night an official called to say they wouldn't be sending me a ribbon. I was bitterly disappointed, but only for a moment. "We can't fit your trophy into your envelope," the secretary explained. The hard work and patience—from rider *and* horse—had paid off.

I changed Kelly's name for shows after that. At home, she's still Kelly, but in competition she's Rubesca—a posh name for what is now a posh horse.

I haven't bothered with a crib collar for years; Kelly has earned the right to indulge her vices. She's never colicked from them, and my other horses haven't picked up the habits. Often, I'm asked why my mount hangs out her tongue during the warmup but not for the test. The answer is simple: I believe she won't, so she doesn't.

That little chestnut has taught me to ride with sensitivity. She makes me look like a competent horsewoman. Together, we've won dressage, show jumping, and combined training competitions in England and in the United States. She loves her work and refuses to retire; at age twenty-four she won a one-day event.

My best moments each day happen when I go into Kelly's stable. She turns her chiseled head to look at me with the most beautiful liquid eyes, brimming with kindness and contentment. How did I ever consider her ugly?

Swollen with pride and happy anticipation, I go out to ride Kelly, the mare who makes me look so good. I tie her to the ring in the wall, and the cat runs along the hayloft above her. Startled, she pulls on her lead rope, breaks free, and gallops down the drive.

When I finally catch up with her, I *swear* that horse is winking at me!

—HILARY C. T. WALKER

A Horse Named Kat

It started when I was twelve. My stepfather left us one day before I woke up for school. As I trudged to the bus stop that morning, I was flooded with shame and worry, but also relief. He never came back; no goodbye to me, no explanation.

Mom had seen my nervous facial tic in Daddy's presence. She had asked him not to yell at me, but my sensitivity and awkwardness frustrated him. If I failed to keep my eye on the ball in miniature golf, aim straight at bowling, or understand his directions for setting up the tent when we went camping, he would yell, "Not like that! What do you think you're doing?" My face would scrunch as I tried not to cry. Only babies were allowed to cry.

Mom signed me up for classes she thought would build my confidence and coordination. I flounced around the house in my tutu and pink ballet slippers and led imaginary parades with my baton, but I never made it to a single recital. When Mom would find me hiding in the back of a class, she would encourage me to participate with the other little girls. She explained to my teachers how shy I was and asked for their patience. But nothing cured the stomachaches, headaches, and diarrhea that forced me to quit before every dreaded performance.

I proved my ineptitude in all things physical time and time again. My lopsided swimming stroke rammed me into the same side of the pool I had just left, which the coach and other kids found hilarious. By sixth grade, I was so convinced of the humiliation awaiting me in gym class that Mom arranged for me to take library instead of physical education.

When Dad moved out, Mom's optimism returned. One month later, a horse trailer pulled up in front of our house in suburban Houston. Kat backed out. He shook himself, looked me in the eye, sniffed my face, and then nodded as if giving me his approval. Silver hairs in his roan coat shone in the sunlight. I fell in love.

Mom was undaunted by the fact that neither of us knew a thing about taking care of a horse—or that we had no place to keep him. Back then you could rent a horse for an hour and ride around a pasture with little supervision. Mom treated me to these rides on my birthdays whenever Dad was away at work. All my experience with horses had been eight or ten rides at those rental stables around Houston.

Kat moved into our backyard and grazed on the thick St. Augustine grass for a week before we found the Greenwoods' stables. We consulted the *World Book Encyclopedia* to figure out how to saddle and bridle him and fed him oats out of the turkey roaster.

I believe that Mom asked St. Jude, the patron saint of impossible causes, to give Kat the power to transform me. More than once that first week I caught her in the backyard talking to the horse and patting his silver neck.

I met three kids my age at the stables the first day: Sissy, Roger, and Joni. I hadn't counted on other people witnessing my ignorance, and Mom blew my plan to watch and learn as much as I could without having to ask for coaching.

"Hi, kids," she said cheerfully. "We don't know much about horses, so I hope you'll teach Lucy the ropes." My face felt scorched. I looked at the ground then peeked at their faces to see their reaction.

"Sure," said Sissy with a gleam in her eye. "We'll teach her everything we know. Won't we guys?"

"Let's go for a ride," Joni said.

I felt stupid climbing into my saddle as they all swung up like monkeys onto their bareback horses.

"Can you handle a lope?" Sissy asked.

"Sure," I said, hoping that a lope wasn't a fast gallop. Kat followed them through the tall grass, his black mane flapping in time with his easy gait. My butt thudded against the saddle. We stopped at Dairy Queen for sodas, and Sissy challenged me to arm wrestle. She slammed my arm down onto the table in three seconds. The next day, she jumped on my back and made me carry her from the driveway to the barn.

I began to sneak out early in the morning to practice swinging up on Kat without an audience. Grabbing a handful of mane, I threw my leg up and clung to his side like a daddy longlegs on the side of a barn as I tried to pull myself up the rest of the way. Again and again I tried, until my arms trembled with fatigue and tears of frustration burned my throat.

When Mom found out that Sissy and Roger lived near us she offered them rides to the stables on her way to work—so much for learning in secret. They encouraged me to ride bareback, and gave me a leg up until I could mount on my own. I slipped from side to side, clenching Kat's girth with my wimpy legs. I was still unsteady when Sissy goaded me into a race. I protested, but Joni and Roger insisted I had to get used to speed if I planned to compete in the Western pleasure horse shows they all loved. I didn't tell them I had no intention of competing in any kind of show ever.

As soon as we lined up, Joni yelled, "Go!"

My breakfast rose in my throat as Kat reared up and charged after Sissy and her black-and-white Paint, Sugar. The heat of Kat's fury radiated through my legs and into my whole body while I clung to his mane with terrified exhilaration.

Each day Mom packed apples and carrots for me to take to Kat, and he, in turn, greeted me like his best friend. Each night, Mom drew hot baths to soothe my aching legs and bottom. She reminded me that working sore muscles made them stronger. When I collapsed under the weight of a fifty-pound sack of feed, Mom fetched a wheelbarrow and helped me hoist the bag into it.

After weeks of riding all day, shoveling manure, and grooming Kat, my body started to change. Unloading hay from a trailer one hot afternoon, I felt my back and shoulder muscles work together to heave the awkward bales into the shadowy loft. Welts had formed on my scratched arms and sweat dripped into my eyes. I felt happier than I could ever remember. Even Sissy couldn't lift a bale of hay alone; she needed my help. The next week I carried the feed over my shoulder instead of in the wheelbarrow. I wobbled and staggered but made it all the way to the barn.

Mr. Greenwood grabbed my bicep and whistled, "Look at them muscles!"

"Almost as big as mine," said Sissy, flexing her arm and then punching me.

On our morning trips to the stable, Mom listened to Roger and Sissy brag about the ribbons they'd won at horse shows. They were practically undefeated in rescue. Dixie, who was fifteen, had beaten them by one-hundredth of a second in the last show, and they were determined to beat her before she moved into the sixteen-and-older age group.

"Isn't that exciting, Lucy?" Mom said. "I can't wait to watch you kids compete."

I rolled my eyes and scrunched down in the seat, but I soon tired of feeling jealous and left out.

I rode Kat into the pen that day and loped him through the barrels. Joni climbed on the fence to watch. "Way to go!" she hollered as we crossed the finish line.

"Really?" I smiled at my saddle.

"Try it again, but lean into the turns more. Just before his withers line up with the barrel."

Kat pawed the dirt at the starting line and tossed his head. He cut so close as he dashed around the barrel that my knee whacked on the rim.

Sissy and Roger joined Joni as my self-designated coaches. They laughed at my clumsy maneuvers and cheered every improvement. I soon asked for tips and followed every word. Sissy announced that Kat and I had the best chance at flags and straightaway barrels. Kat could stop on a dime, but my jerky reining slowed him too much for clover-leaf barrels. As she watched me practice, Mom fingered the rosary in her pocket and silently prayed—for what, I don't know. That I'd hang onto the horse and not be killed as he flung me around the barrels? That the other kids would accept me even if I failed? Or that I'd learn to accept myself and have fun no matter how well I did?

As the first horse show drew near, the old panic churned in my gut. "My stomach hurts," I told Joni. "I may be getting sick."

"We all do before a show. You'll live."

At the Pasadena Rodeo Fair Grounds, my heart pounded in my ears so I could barely hear when the announcer called my name. Kat pranced and tossed his head as we waited in the chute.

"Calm down, or I may throw up," I told him. I clutched a blue flag in my right hand and the reins in my left. The starter gun popped. We shot into the arena toward the first flag in the bucket of sand on the right side of the fence. Kat's hooves pounded the soft dirt and drowned out the sounds of Sissy, Roger, and Joni hollering my name. Afraid of passing the flag, I yanked the reins and Kat skidded to a stop three feet before the bucket. I urged him forward. He danced in a circle. I fumbled, swallowed the lump in my throat, and finally exchanged the flags. Kat flew around the barrel at the end of the arena and raced to the second flag, barely holding still long enough for me to shove the red one in the sand and grab the blue one out. He raced to the finish line heaving big breaths of air, his nostrils flaring, his ears pricked straight ahead. I didn't hear my time. Sissy, Roger, and Joni whooped and hollered as they met us outside the arena.

"You and The Kat were great!" Sissy smacked me on the back when I dismounted.

Roger punched me in the arm.

Joni shoved me. "Ya'll are bound to win a ribbon."

Mom threw her arms around me. "Honey, I am so proud of you."

I didn't win a ribbon that day. I didn't need a ribbon to know I was coordinated enough to ride a horse bareback at a dead run across open fields, or strong enough to carry my own feed, or responsible enough to take care of a horse who depended on me for everything. I didn't need a ribbon to prove that I was brave enough to show up in front of an audience and do my best. I had lots of other chances to win ribbons in the years I owned Kat.

I don't know if Mom believed that a horse could make up for the father who had abandoned me, but Kat did for me what my Dad could never do. I thank Mom to this day for understanding that.

—LUCY S. LAUER

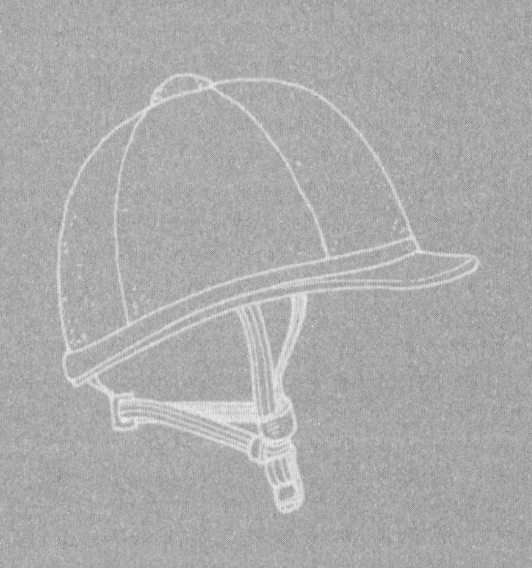

Vieux Chapeau (Old Hat)

Evelyn barely heard the knock over the sounds of the blizzard. With her feet shoved into Derek's old boots, she shuffled across the kitchen's stone floor to answer it.

"Madame Collier, I am sorry to bother . . . " said her neighbor, Monsieur Vuillan.

"Evelyn, *si'l vous plait*," she corrected him.

"*Ah oui,* Eee-va-leen." His five words of English exhausted, he bombarded her with rapid-fire French, engrossed in telling his tale of doom: Derek's prized Merens horses were at risk. Evelyn's other neighbor, Gaston Purbeille, had allowed his meat horses to break their fence—again.

A few years ago Monsieur Vuillan would have been telling this to Derek while she made a flask of coffee for them to take to the fields. But Derek was dead now, and it was up to her. Monsieur Vuillan offered to bring the Merens up to the top field for her, to keep them safe while Gaston tried to reclaim his stock, but he wanted her permission in case anything went wrong. Shaking her head, Evelyn turned to find her own boots. She would bring the horses in herself.

She pulled on her hiking boots and laced them carefully. Then she made a swift mental list of her needs: a torch, gloves, a roll of wire, hammer and fence pins to repair the fence, and a scarf to protect her face. What else? Something that would bring the horses to her. She went into the kitchen and grabbed her old gardening gloves, the ones she now called "horse-gloves."

Evelyn peeled a banana, sprinkled sugar on it, and put it in the microwave for ten seconds. A rich scent wafted: the aroma of tropical holidays and childhood sweets. When it was softened, she squeezed the banana, smearing fruit all over the gloves. Monsieur Vuillan watched in frank amazement. She knew she'd given him a great tale to tell about the crazy Englishwoman. So what? The horses were what mattered. She put the banana-coated gloves in a plastic bag. She pulled on her coat and filled the pockets with her supplies, including the gloves and another bag with an old baguette, stale croissants, and wrinkled apples. She grabbed her slouch hat, too. What had she forgotten? Ah yes, they would need a spare fence battery—Gaston would have switched off the current and moved the battery to another fence; he was too miserly to keep all the fences live. If she left it to him to return his own battery to this fence, the damn meat horses would break through again before he would bother.

As soon as Evelyn stepped out of the doorway, the wind seized her. She rammed her hat down and thrust her free arm out like a one-armed swimmer trying to make headway against the gale. In the shed, she rummaged for wire, wire-cutters, and a fence battery. With the wire slung across her body, cutters in her pocket, and the battery held in one hand, she braved the storm again. The hat fell over her eyes, and she had to clamp her hand to it. Back in the kitchen, she pulled off the hat and glared at it. It obviously wasn't up to the unpredictable French mountain springtime. As she chucked it back on the rack, she saw Derek's fur hat, half-obscured by ancient boots. She smiled. He'd bought that old thing the first year they came to France, before they'd bought the house, before they'd retired here, before he'd died so unexpectedly from a massive coronary eight years ago.

She'd planned to sell the house and the horses after his death. She'd asked Gaston to feed the Merens and sell them, and she'd picked an agent to handle the house sale. Then she went home to England and sat in the little flat that she and Derek had chosen. They had planned on having their real home in France.

Six weeks after the move back to England, Evelyn received a frenzied phone call.

"Vous devez venir que vite que possible!" It sounded as though something terrible had happened, but Evelyn—fighting to decipher the incomprehensible French being hurled at her—knew that with Derek dead, there could be no terrible things. Nothing mattered.

Slowly she unpicked the story. Madame Vuillan was telling her that Gaston was stealing her horses. Evelyn laughed and told Madame Vuillan she'd got it wrong—Gaston was trying to sell them. That brought another torrent. Apparently Gaston was only offering her a quarter of what the buyer would give him for the horses and—much worse—he was trying to get all the mares in foal before he sold them, so that he could keep the foals.

Who cares? Evelyn thought. But she remembered Derek's enthusiasm for his Merens. "They're beautiful little horses, more like ponies," he had said. "They'll do anything you ask them to, and they're an ideal mountain breed: hardy, intelligent, and friendly. You're going to love them, Evie." But horses were not her thing. She liked cooking, walking, and painting—a second home in the French Pyrenees would give her scope for her hobbies.

With the phone call came feelings of shame and guilt. Why had she left Gaston—a farmer whom Derek had despised—to deal with the horses? Why had she abandoned Derek's dream just because he was no longer around? She couldn't do a worse job than Gaston. She decided to go back to France and sell the horses herself.

That first week, Madame Vuillan had driven Evelyn from farm to farm to talk to breeders about the Merens. They'd seen countless little black horses. Then she'd gone down to Gaston's farm and looked at her own troop. Already she could see that Derek had chosen well. His Merens were shiny black and sprightly with lively eyes and well-shaped heads.

"*Ceci c'est Minerve*," said Madame Vuillan, pointing to one horse. Minerva, the boss, the head honchette. Evelyn had looked into the horse's eyes and seen Derek's ambition looking back at her. Madame Vuillan had slipped the head collar onto Minerva, but it was Evelyn who led her back up the mountain to her home—their home.

Min was getting on now. She was nine years old and had given four wonderful foals: three mares and a stallion. There were nine mares in the troop, plus three foals, and a yearling stallion that Evelyn planned to put to stud. He was Min's son and had all her bright grace.

The yearling was the one at risk now. Gaston had a stallion in his fields, getting his brood mares in foal. If that huge male caught scent of Min's son there would be trouble. Her little stallion in the making could end up fighting a horse the size of Goliath. Bloody Gaston!

Evelyn pulled Derek's hat off the floor and jammed it on her head. It looked like a half-bald gray cat with ratty strings dangling like skinny legs, and half-tufted fur sticking out at all angles. She tied the laces under her chin. It might look terrible, but it was warm.

With Monsieur Vuillan in tow, she strode down to the field where the fence had been broken. Gaston jumped as though he'd been scared from his skin when Evelyn appeared out of the blizzard. As she circled on her heel to guess where the horses might be, she heard him mutter to Monsieur Vuillan, "I thought it was Derek's ghost when I saw that old hat." He used the local *patois*—the *Langue d'Oc*—because he knew that she would understand French. But Madame Vuillan spoke the old language too, and had taught Evelyn much of it as they worked together on the horses. Madame Vuillan, in fact, had taught her all she needed to survive, from making fires to filing hooves. When Evelyn asked why, the old woman just shrugged. "Your husband was a good horseman," she said, as though that was an answer. At the end of her first year as a widow, Evelyn had grown vegetables, chopped wood, and groomed horses. She'd burned her watercolor brushes on a December bonfire and never regretted it. Derek had been right: She loved the horses.

Evelyn smiled grimly. She'd had just about enough of Gaston's bad farming. In fact, she'd give him another shock, right now. "Gaston, where are your meat horses?" She yelled, in French, above the storm. He shrugged.

"Okay," she shouted, "I'll bet you I can find your horses and return them to their field in half an hour. What do you think?"

He sneered. "Ha! These aren't Merens, Miss Collier. These are meat horses, to be sold for food. They're untamed—you'll never bring them in."

Wanting to conceal the fear that she might make a fool of herself after all, she smiled back, "I'll bet you a fence battery!"

Monsieur Vuillan intervened, "Take the bet or turn it down, Gaston, I don't want to be out here all day."

Gaston nodded. "Not a hope, Miss, you'll owe me a battery in thirty minutes."

"Madame, Gaston, not Miss. You call me Madame Collier. And now you can get busy. Here's the wire—when I bring them back through, you'd better have that fence repaired."

She wondered what had got into her. It was as though Derek's hat had infected her with his confidence. She'd never made a bet in her life, and leading wild horses through a blizzard wasn't anything she'd ever thought she'd be good at. The new snow crunched under her feet—February snow, damaging to the farm. The new grass that had begun to appear would be blighted. Her feet were freezing. Her head was warm though. She reached up and touched the hat as though for luck, then trudged on. She knew where Gaston's horses would be.

At the field corner where she stopped every day when she'd collected her post, she saw them. They were on the wrong side of the fence—her side instead of Gaston's—but that's where they were, waiting: Seven brood mares, all huge and brown and unnamed, and the stallion. The stallion didn't have a name either. She had nicknamed him Rock Star, because of his muscles, his blond mane, and his lack of brains. For weeks the meat horses had met her in this corner, and she'd fed them old bread and carrots. She had once hated the idea of horses being killed for their meat, but France had taught her that one animal was much like another; she must either turn vegetarian or cry over every lamb chop. She'd come to terms with it. These mares had a good life, and so did Rock Star. Life wasn't so great for their foals, of course, but that was out of her hands.

She pulled on the horse-gloves. From the huddled mass of horseflesh a blonde mane appeared. Rock Star sniffed and pushed his harem out of his way. Evelyn held out her hands. Through the arctic air, the banana scent reached all the horses; they turned like sleepwalkers and came to her.

As they came level, she pulled bits of bread and apples from her pocket. They took the food from her hands as she walked back to the gap in the fence. The horses, smelling ambrosia but getting only plain flavors from the food she gave them, followed her closely, seeking the source of the wonderful fragrance.

Through the storm she saw Gaston and Monsieur Vuillan still bending over the fence posts, hammering the pins. She came past them in a cloud of warm, horse-scented air, her hand on Rock Star's side. Gaston's mouth hung open in shock.

Once in the field she patted the horses. "Good boy," she said to Rock Star. She scratched the biggest brown mare between the eyes, "Good girl, Brunhilde," she said. She had given them all names, she couldn't help herself—the mares were all opera heroines.

She felt something on her head. It was Rock Star, nibbling Derek's hat. She must have rubbed her banana-scented hand over it at some point. The laces held, and the hat stayed firmly on her head.

"A fence battery, remember?" she yelled to Gaston. Monsieur Vuillan applauded with gloved hands. The bet would be paid, or Gaston would be a laughingstock. Either way, Evelyn had done something that would cement her place in the village.

She pushed back up the hill to find her own horses. They stood in the lee of the slope, snow speckling their black coats. Minerva stepped free of the troop to meet her. "Hello Min," she said, "I've just been rescuing those brown giants. You'd never be that silly, would you?" Minerva rested her long nose on Evelyn's shoulder and breathed deeply. "Here, I brought you all something," she said, with her hands full of bread and apples, her head as warm as tea in a pot, despite the snow.

—Kay Sexton

Raising Tagel

As I drive to the barn, my legs make the motions of a musical free-style I'll never perform, a series of tempi changes as I round the corner into the driveway. For years now, I've danced my way to the university where I teach, choreographing detailed dressage routines to favorite songs during the lengthy commute. As a training-level rider in my late forties, I'm well aware that the only Olympics I'll ever compete in are the ones held daily in my car.

It's a sunny mid-October day at the peak of autumn in Pennsylvania, the kind of day that will tempt my students to cut class. I park my car and head to the pasture where Tagel, my five-year-old Oldenburg, grazes with the herd at the barn that I like to think of as his boarding school.

When I talk about my horses to my non-horsey friends, they smile indulgently and suspect my horses are substitutes for "real" offspring. "I desperately want a child," I tell people. Their eyebrows rise when I add, "I just don't want it to be human." For me, the decision to raise an equine family was a choice, made with the same sense of commitment, the same doubts and fears as any move into parenthood. Was it fair to put my mare at risk? Would I be able to handle a young horse?

I delayed the decision, letting one mare purchased for breeding go foal-less. But by the time I reached forty, I could feel my biological clock ticking. I wanted a baby, and waiting until I was older wasn't going to make raising the baby any easier.

I think about these old fears as I walk into the pasture. I call Tagel's name, and he stops grazing, lifts his head, and watches me move closer before he begins to walk over, looking for the carrot he knows is in my hand. I look at him and see not one horse, but a series of horses—all the different versions of him transposed one on top of the other. Although everyone who looks at him remarks on his large size, I still see him as a tiny, delicate foal.

When we had decided to breed, I promised myself I wouldn't become emotionally attached until the baby had all four hooves firmly planted on the ground.

As I lead him back to the barn now, Tagel quietly walks beside me, a major accomplishment of its own. He has always been active—he tried to stand before he was fully out of the birth canal. He has always been friendly—he was perfectly willing to accept my husband as his mother for the first twenty minutes of life while his real one lay exhausted in the stall. My early fears about being a good mother were in many ways justified as I discovered the challenges of inter-species relationships. It took Tagel a year and a half before he understood that I wasn't another horse. He would bump into me the same way he did with them, and offer a kick to the ribs if he wanted to get away to eat grass. All the horse books emphasize a foal's innocence, but he was also a budding stallion. My veterinarian laughed when I told her he would milk from mama one moment and practice his mounting skills on her the next. And he wasn't the least bit shy about trying those abilities out on me, either. One morning as I led him to the pasture, I made the mistake of getting too far in front of him and saw a blur of legs descend over my head.

Our training process means that I have to learn to see the world from his perspective; he has to learn he is different from me. I've often felt a parent's guilt about fears I've thrust on him. During his first trailer ride, at three years old, he entered a box that he didn't really want to go into that then began shaking. When it finally stopped and opened up again, he saw that the whole world had changed. No wonder he didn't want to enter his new stall that day.

When we approach the gate to leave the pasture, we meet Tagel's nemesis, a half-Clydesdale named Jett. I feel Tagel's fear as he slows down. Jett was first to challenge Tagel when he joined the herd. Tagel took one look at him and decided Jett was too much horse for him. He found a yearling with a babysitter gelding, two horses that kept away from the others, and immediately checked himself into the nursery section of the herd. There he stayed for the rest of the summer.

Tagel and I take a few nervous steps, and Jett lets us pass through the gate. I cross-tie Tagel in the barn and begin to brush and tack him up. He stands relatively still, except to paw when I try to put his splint boots on, a baby habit I haven't been able to break.

After Tagel was born, I read every equine version of Dr. Spock I could find, did imprint training, and went to horse-handling seminars. Still, there were times when he seemed impossible.

When Tagel was a yearling I called a farrier who billed himself as a local horse whisperer. The man picked up one of Tagel's front legs, and at the first sign of resistance let loose a string of four-letter words that echoed through the surrounding hills. Embarrassed, he said it was his way of relieving frustration, rather than taking it out on the horse.

The horse-swearer was quickly replaced by a woman farrier, who traveled with five dogs. As we walked down the hill toward the barn during her first visit, the dogs running at our sides, I was certain we were headed toward disaster. Four-letter words at ear-shattering decibels now made Tagel even more nervous about having his feet picked up, and he had never seen a dog. To my surprise, he was so fascinated by the dogs that he ignored the farrier, allowing her to do whatever she wanted.

Once Tagel is tacked I lead him to the arena. Although shy about approaching the mounting block, he stands nicely as I get on. I remember the expression on his face the first time he saw me get on another horse. He was being weaned and was running free in the arena while I rode his companion gelding. As I mounted the other horse, Tagel's eyes widened, and he stretched his nose out toward us. He looked away as though in disbelief, then looked back, his eyes widening even more. Then he made a motion that was as close to a horse shrugging its shoulders as I can imagine. If it was okay with his babysitter, then it was okay with him. The gelding and I trotted off, and Tagel followed along behind.

Being mounted was something Tagel accepted from the very start, but having his rider come off at the end of the ride was a different story. The reappearance of his trainer next to him was the most startling part of Tagel's first few weeks under saddle. Calm at the start, he'd grow increasingly tense, waiting for the moment when a person was suddenly going to fall out of the sky.

We walk around the arena to warm up, and I think about our progress. Two winters ago my husband took a picture of Tagel with his back legs kicked up so high he was nearly standing vertical, his own buck practically sending him head over heels. "So you're going to put a saddle on that," my husband laughed.

Tagel's ultimate surprise was how gentle he turned out to be. We can walk, trot, and canter to the left. So far only the right canter has eluded us. We can make a wobbly circle or two but we're awkward and unbalanced, not quite comfortable with each other. As we walk around I listen to the leaves rustle around us and feel the warmth of the sun. After a few minutes we trot, work circles and serpentines, and focus especially on the bend to the right, his difficult direction. We canter to the left. I think about him and his movement as we ride, and the quiet pleasure of the day itself. And then, suddenly, we pick up a nice smooth canter to the right. For the first time, a motion that had eluded us for weeks comes both easily and naturally. As we circle around I can feel my body moving with his, anticipating his motions. It's not perfect by any means, but it's the beginning of a partnership.

We stop and look over the fields, and I'm aware of him underneath me, looking in the same direction, enjoying the same moment. There are no cheering crowds, no ribbons to be won, but I know this is the moment I'll always look back on and think, we made it. I managed to raise Tagel to some version of horse adulthood. The fact that no one is here to witness it is somehow appropriate. The closeness between horse and rider is ultimately something private, to be felt on a good ride, on a good day, when we forget for a moment that there is a world beyond the two of us.

I get off and lead him back to the barn. He seems extra affectionate, nuzzling me rather than offering his usual baby bites. In half an hour, I'll be headed to work to face the students who will have dragged themselves reluctantly to class. But I'll go to work with a sense of elation, my legs performing their imaginary choreography with extra vigor. I wouldn't trade a real Olympic victory for the one I just had—a simple canter on a horse I raised myself, and the moment I finally believed I'm a good mom.

—Carole Waterhouse

Home after Dark

In apple blossom time, Lance would not let himself be caught, but would spring around the paddock like a long-legged cat bouncing through the grass. He'd toss his head back and forth, then drop to his knees in a pile of dust. With a grunt and a sigh, he'd roll over, flailing sharp hooves like dangerous castanets every which way in the sun. Sitting on his haunches, he'd boost up splay-legged and shake.

He'd let the bridle go on then, letting himself be curry-combed back to his gleaming red self. Head low in dreamy pleasure, he'd let his tail be picked out until it fell in a black calligraphy to his hocks. When he was beautiful again, we'd tear up through the apple blossom alley and plunge knee-high through blue foothills of indigo lupine. When sunflowers bloomed, his legs would be golden to the belly in pollen; we ran through fields of wild phlox, his hooves shone with sunset shades of coral and lipstick.

When we crossed the Wenatchee River, strings of algae caught on his churning hooves and then slipped away into the dark current. The smell of river water steaming from horseflesh burned itself into my scent memory. I would stretch out on the sand, and

Lance would put his face down on my face. His breath smelled of last summer's hay, and it still drifts across my face when I am anxious, needing a horse to lean on.

When I was a young girl and Lance was a young horse, Valentine's Cabin was as far as we went during the week. The old Valentine coal mine was boarded up, but the lean-to roof still stood to give shade to kids and rattlesnakes. I liked to ride straight up the ridgeline, Lance lunging, me hanging on by my knees and a double wrap of mane around a fist. Because I rode bareback, often I floated out in space in these near-vertical ascents, barely touching down as Lance buckled and climbed in a muscled flow beneath me.

Eventually, I would shorten the reins, sit sharply back, and bring his head in, slowing him with his utmost reluctance to a jolting trot. My favorite place was in the orchard, though, where the grass grew soft and green. I read in the dappled shade while the rhythm of Lance's cropping lulled me into believing this was the only world I'd ever know.

Above us was Horse Lake itself, no more than a holding pond for watering cattle. Still, it was somewhat of a feat to ride the ridge way up to the Barnhill's ranch and beyond to the lake. I rarely saw anyone up there, but the Barnhills knew I was one of the Brown girls who lived down by the river. Old Mrs. Barnhill would wave from the front porch of her weathered farmhouse, and a ranch hand would appear to help me with the heavy gate closure. I would wave or stammer my shy thanks.

One September day, with the tang of apple harvest in our nostrils, the shake of first gold glinting through the high-swaying cottonwoods, Lance and I left the lowlands to ascend the steep ridge north of Saddle Rock.

Lance was in a mood for climbing. We came to the power lines and paused. Lance puffed his big bay chest between my knees and tugged at the reins for grazing slack. We were so high up I could see the Columbia glinting north to the curve below Rocky Reach Dam, south to the basalt columns above Rock Island Dam. To the northwest, I could see the Wenatchee and the curve where my family lived, a half-mile from its confluence with the central stem, Great Mother Columbia.

I heard a hum in the air, vibrating from the rock I lay on. I moved my arms behind me and leaned back to look up at the giant metal structures that strung cables from the dam generators east across the Columbia Plateau, west over the Cascades to light the coastal cities.

Lance butted my arm with his white blaze, ready to go. He spoke with his red and black ears, flipping them in semaphore. I got on the uphill side of him, made a flying leap, grabbed at his mane, and landed far back on his hindquarters as he headed enthusiastically uphill.

Lance and I both felt the pull, a restless attraction to an indefinite journeying. We approached the timberline at a place I'd never been before. Under the big Douglas firs, we paused, surprised by the dropping temperature. The road led faintly between the trees. Chirring chipmunks broke the silence.

Deeper and higher I rode into the trees. We branched onto several sidetracks, traveled across icy meadows with their brief sunlight. In a clearing we stopped. We had met no one, and had encountered only tracks of deer, coyote, and raccoon.

I let Lance tear at the grass for a while; I stretched full length along his spine and smelled his sweat rising. I felt clear as a pane of glass. Light shone through us both.

I thought about the lateness of the hour and wondered where we were exactly. I wasn't lost. I was pretty sure if we cut through trees to the north, we'd come out a mile or two above Horse Lake and could turn east down the switchbacks once we'd crossed Barnhill's ranch. This story is not about getting lost. My father taught us to pay attention to where we were. I knew that all trees did not look alike. I knew how to follow my tracks home or water downhill. This story is not about getting thrown off Lance because I have never been thrown from a horse. Mom likes to remind me of the time Lance and I encountered a pack of motorcycles coming down Horse Lake Road, how Lance squealed, reared, spun on his back legs, galloped wildly to the bottom of the hill, and made a ninety-degree turn up into the creek bed. I stuck to him like Velcro she said, and it's true, Lance made demon riders out of us kids.

This story is not about a rattlesnake striking Lance in the leg. That happened another time when my sister Toren was riding. I remember looking out the window at midnight and seeing by light of the Coleman lantern my sister Cheryl's blonde head bent over Lance's hugely swollen leg as she changed a cool poultice for a hot one. His neck was curved around to watch, eyes full of curiosity and pain. Her silver pin shaped like a running horse, with a spirit line of opal running from neck to tail, caught a wink of lantern light.

This story is about the dreaming strange safety of a child and an animal guide. It's true that behind the poplar trees on the cliff was a man who liked to pick peaches in the nude and who exposed himself to me when I went up to his house to be paid for orchard work. It's true the apples were sprayed with Parathion. It's true that between the stars and us blew downwind radiation from the Hanford nuclear plant. I can look back through the anxious lens of time knowing the worst that is possible for a young girl alone, bareback on a large and spirited animal in the distant hills away from home, but this story is not about that world.

I pulled Lance's head up and threaded him through the trees at an angle. He didn't object, so I knew I wasn't too far off. He picked up another snowy, muddy road and followed it downhill—his contribution to path finding. It was a good one, too, because the path moved into the open and became the trace beginnings of Horse Lake Road. The gilded evening light ruffled Barnhill's field of late wheat as if it were water. Cattails hid the muddy banks of Horse Lake. Seed heads had partially burst, so clouds of backlit fluff drifted in front of us. Lance snorted and tossed them with his nose until they scattered into the incandescent flame of the standing wheat.

At the Barnhill's, we were brought up short by the closed gate. I slipped off Lance and struggled with the tightly strung pole and wire contraption. By wiggling and pushing, I got enough leverage to slip the wire off the post. I dragged back the fence and led Lance through, but I couldn't get it shut. It had been built for adult men to close, not thirteen-year-old girls.

I led Lance to the farmhouse. In the window I could see an ultraviolet grow light over a double shelf of African violets. The tiny flowers with fuzzy leaves glowed eerily periwinkle under the peculiar blue light. Mrs. Barnhill answered the door but was unconcerned about the open gate. "I'll send one of the boys out. Don't you worry. It's getting late—you get on down the road."

I led Lance up alongside the porch and jumped on him from there. He sidled away, but I had my double twist of black mane and straightened up under his sideways movement. We headed down the three miles of switchbacks, the sun immediately dropping below the horizon as we descended into the canyon. Lance walked slowly, like a tired old man with his head down. When the road switched at the cliff edge, we paused to watch shadows gather over the Wenatchee River, which remained a sinuous run of silver mercury long after dark.

At the two-mile mark, I saw headlights start up the hill, disappearing and reappearing as the vehicle made the steep turns. When its lights picked me out, it parked at the overlook, engine idling. It was my father in our orange International Travel-All. He got out, came over and patted Lance on his shoulder. "Have a good ride?" he asked, "Getting kind of dark."

"We were up above the lake, "I said. "It was farther than I thought."

He looked at the starry skyline over my shoulder. "Ten miles, maybe twenty round-trip. That's a full day. Dinner's held for you." He patted Lance one more time, got in the Travel-All, and drove slowly down the hill ahead of me.

When Lance and I got home, I forked out a couple slabs of the summer-scented hay, measured oats, and rubbed him down while he ate. He was almost asleep on his feet when I left him, but he followed me with one half-opened eye as I let myself out the gate. Tomorrow, he'd be tossing his head by the whitewashed corral fence, whinnying and running back and forth, ready to go.

Later, Mom would say she had gotten worried when I hadn't returned by suppertime and had sent Daddy out to look for me. I wasn't scolded, and Daddy never gave a clue he'd been doing anything up the canyon that night except taking in the view. I've never forgotten how far away I rode into a distant land of snow, arriving home after dark. I had grown at once wilder and more calm. The spirit of the horse had entered me like a clear line of opal through a silver pin, pure and full of light.

—SANDY JENSEN

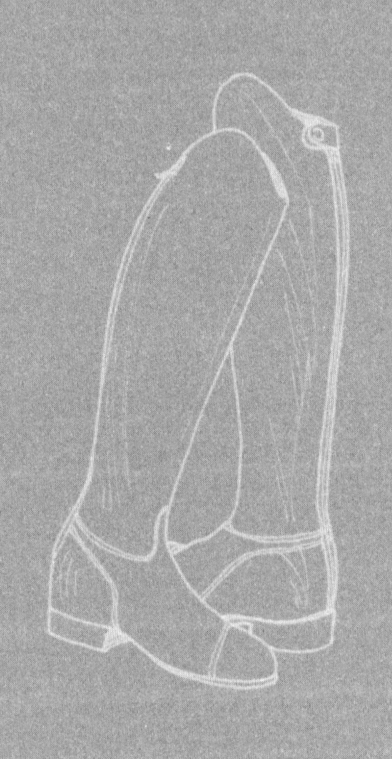

The Biggest Step

Two years. That's how long it had been since the last time I'd put my foot in a stirrup. Two years since I'd ridden Snake. Two long years with me in a back brace, watching him run wild in the pasture. Was I crazy, or was he the perfect horse to help me recover?

Four years ago, I had almost missed the small "prospective barrel horse for sale" ad. His owner was delighted I hadn't. A horse already saddled when a buyer arrives is always a tipoff: Invariably, the horse will be hard to catch, hard to saddle, or hard to handle. Snake was all three. His owner wouldn't ride him, excusing himself with an old injury and lack of skill on a horse that quick. Snake was quick, all right. Quick to snort, quick to pull away, and quick to let me know I wasn't welcome to put my foot in his stirrup. I did anyway. His attempt to run was foiled by a short left rein, and his momentum swung me aboard. I expected him to buck. He didn't, but his ears laid back. He flinched every time I moved. I quit moving. He stood stock still, except for his head—he held it high, turning first left, then right, eyeballing me, wanting to know what was next. I thought about nudging him forward. Just the thought produced the right result. Or did I move ever so slightly? I wasn't sure.

He didn't have a flat walk. He bounced, not quite a prance, certainly not a trot. We moved off in a quick change of pace, fluid, high-stepping, strong. Soon we were loping, then galloping. The wind stung my eyes and sang in my ears. His speed was effortless. His nostrils weren't flaring. His head wasn't even fully extended. I asked for more and got it. He took my breath away.

The end of the arena was approaching fast. I tried to stop him. Leaning toward the left, I intended to use a big circle to gradually slow him down, but he reacted before I could touch the reins. His turn was sharp and clean and almost sent me sailing from the saddle—a perfect barrel-sized arc. I let him go again, and then shifted slightly to the right. Same tight, beautiful turn each time, every time. But no stop. The bit was dead in his mouth. Eventually we did communicate enough to make a wide circle and gradually slow to a stop. I swung off before he could change his mind.

"Wow, he works perfect for you." It wasn't a sales tactic. His owner was truly surprised.

Snake hadn't worked for me. Not really. I'd simply let him do what he wanted, providing cues for what I wanted when I wanted it. Fortunately, he wanted to run and turn. I only stayed aboard with his permission. I knew that and so did he. Was that enough for a partnership? I wasn't sure.

I pulled off the saddle and bridle and turned him loose before the owner could protest. Surprised, Snake rolled his eyes but stood his ground. I ran my hand along his neck and back. He wondered what I was doing, his ears flitted, his head turned back and forth. I reached for his fetlock. He lifted it for me before I touched his leg. But touching his head was forbidden. I wasn't allowed to touch it, not even for a moment. I could see why. Slightly in front of his left eye, angling in and up toward his forehead, was a long, thin indention. Someone had tried to tame his wildness with a pipe. I hoped they paid dearly for their cruelty.

Buoyed by Snake's cooperation, his owner tried to raise the price. I left empty-handed, but he had my number. It was six months before he used it. He was willing to accept his original price if I was willing to pick Snake up that day. When I arrived, the horse was in a five-acre pasture. The price was halved when his owner admitted he couldn't catch him. With the bill of sale safely in my pocket, I gathered hay from the trailer manger and tossed it into the fall-apart catch pen. I sat back and waited. First the ponies came running, then Snake, afraid he was missing something special. I shut the gate behind him, hoping he didn't know how loose the fence rails were. That was the easy part. It took another hour before I could lay the lead rope across his neck and another half hour before the halter was buckled. But he loaded just fine, and we were on our way.

Each day was the same. Every time I cornered him, he'd wheel away to the right, never kicking, never trying to hurt, but always determined to stay free. Only when he tired of the game was I allowed to touch him. It took half an hour to catch him in a stall, another half an hour to put the halter on. Saddling him was another adventure. He would stand frozen, allow me to ease the pad and then the saddle into place. He would snort when I pulled the cinch and buck in place when I added the breast collar. Through all this, he never touched a wall or pulled on the rope. He simply used the space he had, no matter how small, to accomplish his acrobatic feats. The bridle was worse. He accepted the bit easily enough but the headstall couldn't go over his ears. I eased the unbuckled headstall over low on his neck then slid it forward, buckling it quickly before he could dodge away.

The hysterics ended once I swung aboard. He was all business then, waiting to know what the day's tasks were. He was an accomplished rope horse. He could handle the sassiest colt when used for ponying. He was surefooted on the trail and great at working cattle. But barrel racing was what he loved most. At first glance, our competitors didn't take him seriously. His mane was as wild as he was; the feathers on his fetlocks remained long and thick because of his fear of clippers. His Roman nose coarsened his head, and his chest was narrow. The prettiest thing about him was his rich chestnut coat, broken only by a star on his forehead. He looked and acted every inch the range horse, perhaps a mustang, but his origins were unknown except for the heart-lazy-J brand on his shoulder. How could such a rough steed outrun their sleek quarter horses? It only took one event before they paid attention and two before he gained their respect. It wasn't long before he was drawing crowds at the local events. He didn't slow down and rate the barrels; he hit them at full speed. The crowds came to see him drag my stirrup through the dirt as we rounded each barrel, to watch with bated breath as he laid hard into every turn, almost parallel to the ground yet never slipping. They loved watching the timers jump out of his way when we turned our big circle at the end, slowing gradually before bouncing out of the arena in that animated walk of his.

Snake became the leading contender for the year, the horse to beat. The photographers hated him. He would pin his ears back, head turning side-to-side to catch my slightest desire, spoiling their idea of a great win picture. No presenter was brave enough to come near, so not many of his pictures graced the local publications.

And then the accident: No, not an accident; my ex-husband crippled me on purpose. He tossed me into the fireplace hearth as casually as Snake tossed his mane. The doctors weren't sure I'd ever walk again, let alone ride. I vowed to do both. I couldn't imagine life without my horses. Ironically, the fight had been over Snake. My ex had a new gal and she wanted a barrel horse. He thought Snake would be the perfect gift to woo her with. I laughed, knowing he was terrified of my horse. My ex couldn't stand the mockery and resorted to his old standby—violence—to get what he wanted. But it didn't work. Snake wasn't going anywhere without me.

So two years passed. Snake browsed the high grass while I struggled to walk. Not one for small talk, he never came to the pasture fence to visit. He kept his distance, head high, gaze fierce, waiting for me to tell him what I wanted. I didn't want anything except to know he was there, that one day I'd ride him again. Everyone urged me to sell him and get a calmer horse. It would be safer, they said. I couldn't expect to ride like I used to. They didn't understand that selling him was unthinkable. He was my hope. The memory of the wind in my face, tears in my eyes, the sheer glory of those wild runs were all that kept me going. If I was going to win the struggle, our partnership had to be my jackpot.

I spent those years watching him feast on life. Still young, he dominated the other horses, bedeviling them when he wanted, huddling close, tails engaged in mutual fly-chasing when he desired. He romped and ran, sunfishing, twisting his belly high as he leapt off the ground, landing with a bone-jarring intensity. I could feel his power in my bones as I sat wondering if I would have courage when the time to ride finally came. Would he consent to be mine again or would he be forever wild? I was both eager and in dread.

The day arrived. The stirrup was in front of me. The preliminaries were exactly the same: whirling away when I tried to catch him, flinching away when I haltered him, bucking when I added the breast collar. I touched the long indention on his face, thinking of the courage he mustered the first time we met and every time I asked him to give me his all.

I stepped to his side, tightened the left rein, and placed my foot in the stirrup. We stood like that for an eternity, he wondering what I was going to do and when I was going to do it. Fear made me weak. Despair made me stay. What if there were no tomorrows with the wind in my hair? I couldn't bear to have come so far and to get no further. Even if I was thrown, I had to find out: Was he my partner, or was it all for naught?

"I need to borrow your bravery," I whispered and hoped he understood. I wiggled my left foot back to life and tensed in an effort to mount. As always, he moved but this time he circled tight without resistance, lifting me easily into the saddle, then stood still, head turning, waiting for my cue. We rode off as if we hadn't missed a day.

—Loretta Kemsley

If Wishes Were Horses

When I found myself starting my life over from scratch at the age of forty-six, I made myself a wish list in honor of my birthday:

1. House
2. Horse
3. Husband

I wrote those three wishes down on a small Post-it and stuck it to my computer monitor, where they would challenge me every day. With two kids grown and gone and the third entering junior high school, it was time for me to get a life—one that did not revolve around work and kids. When I tried to imagine what that would look like, out popped "The Three H's." The house and the husband didn't surprise me—or anyone else. It's what eludes you in life that you most desire. But the horse?

"It sounds dangerous," my mother told me when she called to wish her aging only child a happy birthday. "Look what happened to Christopher Reeve."

"That was a freak accident, Mom. Besides I'm not going to be competing in any jumping competitions. We're talking a couple of riding lessons. For beginners."

My best friend Sandy wasn't very supportive either. "Aren't you a little old for horseback riding?" she asked over a celebratory glass of pinot grigio at my so-called birthday dinner.

"Happy birthday to me," I answered, raising my glass.

"I mean, aren't horses a little girl's thing? You're not ten years old any more." Six years my senior, Sandy was determined that I should age gracefully, as she was doing.

"How true," I said aloud, and thought, From now on I'll keep the riding lessons to myself.

But it was too late. My mother told my father, and he called me to talk to about it when she was out shopping. Surprisingly, the Colonel was encouraging.

"You could use a hobby," Dad said. "Maybe you'll meet a nice cowboy."

God bless him. Even after all these years, the Colonel still held out hope that I'd meet a *real* man. Maybe he was right. With any luck I could check off both horse and husband in a single trip to a local stable. I called and made an appointment for the next day.

I drove through the Santa Cruz Mountains to Felton on a long, winding road lined with tall pines and redwoods. The facility consisted of a couple of long horse barns, an outdoor arena, and an indoor arena nestled in a neat clearing a quarter-mile off the main road. Woods made up the rest of the property; trails ran in and around the densely forested perimeter.

Pam, the trim young woman who ran the stable, gave me the grand tour of the place, introducing me to the other staff as well as many of the students. Not one student or instructor was over the age of twenty-five. I had children older than these girls—and I said so.

"We have lots of older riders," Pam told me. "You'll do fine." She handed me a helmet and walked me down the barn to the last stall on the left. There stood a large gray gelding, noticeably swaybacked.

"This is Butch," she said. "He used to race."

Butch looked no more like a racehorse than I looked like a supermodel. "How old is he?" I asked.

"Seventeen. But don't let that fool you. He's got some kick in him yet."

So do I, I thought, and smiled at Butch. I wouldn't hold his swayback against him if he didn't hold my less-than-firm thighs against me.

Pam pointed to the grooming kit, and Butch's bit and saddle. "Let's get you ready to ride."

The next half hour was spent teaching an old dog (me) new tricks (picking out Butch's hooves, slipping on the bit and bridle, saddling him up). I tend to be a klutz even when I know what I'm doing, so I needed some serious coaching. Pam was endlessly patient, as was Butch, who stood there quiet as stone while I managed to get everything wrong the first, second, and—in the case of the bit—third time.

The bit scared me. As did Butch's huge horse teeth. The last time I'd seen either was when I was ten years old. Promised a horse by the Colonel when we were stationed in Oklahoma, I'd had to settle for riding lessons in Germany when we were unexpectedly transferred overseas. None of the instructors at the stable spoke English, and the only horse-related words I knew in German were *Pferd* (horse) and *bissen* (to bite). When I asked the stable boy, "*Pferd bissen?*" he shouted, "*Ja, Ja. Achtung! Achtung! Pferd bissen.*" Thirty-five years later, I realized he was probably joking, but at the time it scared the hell out of me. I never went back.

Butch, however, did not seem to be a biting *Pferd*. He suffered my awkwardness with a grace befitting the noble steed he was. I led him to the outdoor area, and he followed along behind me as cheerfully as a puppy. He didn't even balk when I tried, unsuccessfully, to place my foot in the stirrup and pull myself onto the saddle. Three times. Finally Pam brought me a stool. I hoisted myself up.

Once astride my beloved Butch—already I thought of him as my beloved Butch—I was inordinately proud of myself. Ha! Here I am, well-mounted on seventeen hands worth of horse. A curse on the naysayers!

Pam showed me how to work the reins, and how to nudge Butch into a walk and slow trot. I bounced up and down, wildly out of sync with Butch. He didn't seem to mind, but my thighs sure did. Within fifteen minutes, I was exhausted.

Pam smiled. "You might want to do lunges and *pliés* at home. It'll help you give you the strength you need for proper posting."

I dismounted and led Butch back to his stall. Pam gave me a quick lesson in grooming. I was better at this. Having spent much of my life cleaning kids, clothes, and houses, cleaning a horse was a piece of cake. And I loved this part, back in the barn, the smell of the fresh hay, the feel of firm horseflesh, the gleam of Butch's glossy gray coat.

"He likes you," Pam said, approvingly.

I grinned. *He likes me! He really likes me!* My first lesson could not have ended on a happier note. I was hooked on horses, and hooked on Butch.

For the next several months, Butch and I spent a lot of time together. We trotted; we cantered; we galloped. We learned dressage; we rode trails. We held our own with the other—younger—students and horses. It was truly a symbiotic relationship—I gave him apples and sugar cubes; he gave me firmer thighs and a tighter butt.

"You know," Pam told me one day, "you could always lease Butch. You'd be his only rider."

"You've got a deal." I was thrilled. *House, horse, husband*—not necessarily in that order.

"We'll start after Christmas vacation," Pam said. "We'll be closed for three weeks, till after New Year's."

A horse for Christmas! I was so excited. The Colonel gave me new riding boots and a beautiful velvet riding helmet; I bought Butch new duds to match—a new barn blanket and fancy socks. I couldn't wait to get to the stables and start the new year right: on the back of a horse. My horse.

I was at the stables early that cold Saturday morning. Fog was thick through the mountains, and covered the little clearing. I could barely make out the barn. Once inside, I headed straight for Butch's stall, his new barn blanket in my arms and sugar cubes in my pocket.

It was empty. I figured they must have moved him to his new digs, digs that I was now paying for. I decided to ask Pam—and as if by telepathy, she materialized behind me.

"Where's Butch?"

She stood uncertainly at the front of the stall, looking down at the ground. "I'm so sorry," she said. "Butch is gone."

"Gone where?"

"Gone . . ." She hesitated. "We had to put him down."

My arms tightened around the barn blanket. "How?"

"He tripped on a trail ride and broke a leg. There was really nothing we could do. He was pretty old, and . . . " She looked at me. "You can ride Harrison today. When you're ready, we can talk about your leasing another horse."

I nodded, and followed Pam to Harrison's stall. Harrison was an Arabian, as sensitive as a cat, and a joy to ride. But it wasn't the same. I missed Butch.

I didn't go back to the stable after that; the dotcoms started going under and mine was one of them. I got a new job, relocated to the East Coast, and put my riding boots and helmet in storage. When I finally bought a little bungalow on the South Shore of Boston, I found myself in the middle of horse country once again.

House, horse, husband. I unpacked my helmet and riding boots and displayed them in my mudroom, where they'd remind me that a horse beats a husband any day. I'd find the right horse—it was just a question of time—and when I did, Butch would be smiling.

—PAULA MUNIER

Merlin

Last year was a bad year. In March my husband of forty years was diagnosed with cancer, and he was gone by mid-April. By June I'd had facial surgery and radiation therapy for skin cancer. By August I felt better, but then, in September, my brother lost his long fight with cancer. By the time I returned from his funeral in October, my back began to give me serious trouble. November found me walking with a cane and barely able to move about the house because of collapsed vertebrae. I had also developed osteoporosis. I felt badly out of sorts, out of touch, and out of shape. By Christmas the injury had healed, although I was now three inches shorter.

As I learned what to do to keep the bone problem under control, I knew that exercise—weight bearing as well as aerobic—was in order. What I needed was an activity outside of the house—something very different from what I had been doing—sitting. I learned about the National Center for Equine Facilitated Therapy from a pamphlet. The center provides horseback therapy for people with disabilities, and it always needs volunteers. It appealed to me to make a connection with horses again after many years. I was happy to sign up as a sidewalker in therapy sessions. I wasn't entirely certain I could walk for a whole afternoon, or that I was strong enough to manage older kids. I came to Woodside for therapy, just like the clients—and for the horses. In hippotherapy, the driven horse does not see the driver. He relies on the driver's voice, the lines, and the touch of the short whip for instruction. With the therapist on one side and the sidewalker on the other, the rider is often doing exercises or playing games on the horse's back. The therapy horse must ignore everything except the commands of his driver.

In my earliest recollection, I am sitting on a black wooden rocking horse. We lived in suburban Chicago. No one in my family was an admitted horse person, but my mother supported my infatuation. She read to me from the classics, *Smokey the Cow Horse*, *Black Beauty*, Felix Salten's *Florian*. When I could read, I located the shelves to visit in the library, for I knew that horses lived in books.

One day I was sidewalking with a three-year-old boy named Robert. He was perched on a black-and-white pony named Merlin, and the therapist walked on the other side. She gently arranged Robert's stiff legs; he had settled awkwardly on the thick pad held in place by a leather surcingle. As she prompted Robert to sit tall, I nervously tried not to interfere, but kept my arm across his knee to be sure he didn't topple over. Robert didn't talk, but he smiled broadly and leaned forward to grasp Merlin's shaggy mane. I had to nudge Robert back so that he didn't fall over onto the pony's neck.

Our group walked slowly so that there was just enough motion for Robert to have to constantly adjust to it. Merlin followed the horse handler's, Benedicte's, instructions. She drove him on long lines while walking close behind, just touching his long black tail. His furry ears tipped slightly forward, his nose down as he mouthed the bit gently. He was relaxed and seemed to go all by himself, as if the slow stroll up and down the arena was entirely his own idea. In spite of the child playing, talking, and moving on his back, the therapist's commands, and my cheering Robert on, Merlin only paid attention to Benedicte. She chirped, and he moved a bit faster; she gathered in one line just a little, and he turned just a little. This pleased me, for I have had a small hand in re-educating Merlin. I have come back to an old feeling, which is very hard to explain: the connection, the possibility of dialogue with an animal.

After World War II, we moved to a place in the country near Philadelphia. This was horse country. The neighbors had horses, my friends at school had horses, and my family had horses. I was on horseback every day for the next several years. I went to a riding camp in the summers. I rode my own horse as well as the neighbors' horses. There were fox hunts and horse shows, and eventually I was riding for different stables. Those days ended when I went to college; horses were put on hold for a while.

During those years of privilege when I was growing up, I never thought of riding as a possible profession. Later, when I was out in the world and on my own, I would go back to horses more than once to make a living.

Merlin was once a child's show pony; now he's no longer sound enough for the job. When I first started volunteering at NCEFT, they weren't using Merlin because he wasn't reliable. He tended to overreact to distractions, and he was certain that a raised hand or raised whip meant, "GO Merlin!" Fast responses are not useful in therapy horses. Furthermore, he hated having the long lines along his sides and someone always crowding behind him.

One day, I was sidewalking with one of the larger therapy horses, and getting a sore shoulder and neck. For half an hour I had to walk, look up, and hold onto a child who sat higher than my shoulder. I asked Odette at the barn why they didn't get adorable little Merlin into the program. He was the perfect size for the sidewalker helping the child on his back. (I didn't mention my weakness for cute black-and-white ponies.) "Not enough time," was her reply. "He needs a lot more practice."

"I can come and help," I said, suddenly alert to a chance to do more with the horses while staying within my obvious limitations.

It was settled. I would meet her once or twice a week to practice with Merlin. I walked alongside, fussing with an imaginary rider, while Odette drove him, squeezing his sides with the lines; and he walked with his head up and a very worried look on his face. But he walked. And even though he never showed any inclination to bolt, he was tense and unhappy. He was improving, though.

After we got married, Joe and I settled down to raising a family. At first I thought I could have it all: I would get back to riding, raise our children, work part time, and keep house. Eventually there were four children and sundry cats and dogs, but no horses.

When my second daughter, Vera, was in high school, she joined a vaulting class where a local pony club met. They needed help with the horses, so we both worked for the Sundance Vaulters, lunge lining and exercising the vaulting horses. Vera loved it, and so did I, but soon she was off to college, and I found a more serious job.

One day Odette was too busy to work with Merlin, so I worked him alone. It was the first time I'd had a horse on a lunge line since 1981. I let him walk and trot around me, and then, very cautiously, I coaxed him into a canter. I made a point of waggling the whip and waving my arms harmlessly to show him those actions meant nothing to him. He was a quick study, and he began to relax. My regular job that summer, whenever there was a break in therapy sessions, was to mellow Merlin to take "Go!" out of his vocabulary. When I first started volunteering; I was awkward and inept. The horses all seemed taller than I remembered. I was not sure I could control even an old pony on a line. But every time I worked Merlin, I noticed a slight improvement in him and a slight improvement in myself.

Now Merlin is being eased into the therapy program. That is good for Merlin. He was facing an uncertain future if NCEFT didn't use him. That is good for me. Where else would you find an old pony needing reassurance and an old lady so happy to have the chance to work him?

Today I imagine that Merlin looks happier, even when he's in his paddock. I feel stronger and taller as soon I start down the hill from the parking lot. By the time I have walked as far as the barn, I am fitter than I was last week. I know that I still have unfinished business with horses. Together, Merlin and I will figure out just what that is.

—Kay George

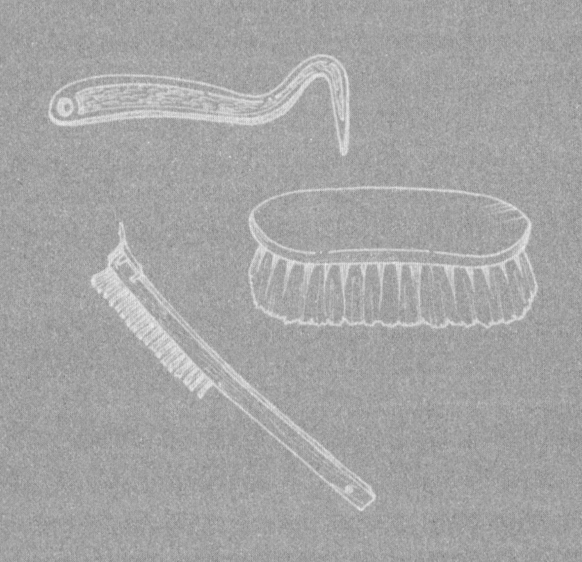

The Horse of My Dreams

I didn't hear anything the old cowboy said. I left the listening to my mother while I gazed at the beautiful chestnut gelding he was holding by the rough rope halter. All I could see was the horse of my dreams, the rich red color of cranberries at Christmas, standing there, dazzling, mine for the taking. I ached to slide over his back into a featherweight English saddle and feel his muscles bunch as we flew over fences in front of cheering crowds. I could see, feel, and taste what it would finally be like to be the one that others envied.

From my first pony ride at age two, from my first deep inhalation of the sweet scent of hay and sweat and saddle soap, I was a horse-crazy girl. Dresses and hair ribbons held no magic for me (I was known to tear the heads off Barbie dolls), but I did harbor a secret passion for the color pink.

As the old cowboy droned on and my mother looked doubtful, I dreamed of replacing the prickly rope halter with a soft, pink nylon one, and placing a pink blanket on my magnificent horse's back and clean pink standing wraps around his fetlocks.

When the man finally stopped talking, my mother looked down into eyes that shone with hope and excitement. She looked at the horse and back at me. "Let's take a walk," she said.

I knew she didn't doubt my ability to ride. I had earned my own riding lessons for over a year, and my instructor said that I had a knack for it—a talent. I knew that my mother wanted to give me the only thing I had ever really wanted. I never wavered, never complained about using my Saturdays for cleaning stalls in exchange for lessons. And I knew that a free horse was a once-in-a-lifetime opportunity. We were always on a tight budget, and as a single parent, my mom could never ever afford this any other way.

"There is a reason he's free, you know," she started. "He's had a hard life, and he hasn't known much kindness."

"That's *perfect*, Mom, he *needs* me," I blurted. "I will love him and take care of him and brush him every day and give him carrots." Then with a flash of inspiration, I added, "We have to *save* him." Now confident that I'd stumbled on the right argument, I continued, "We always take in abandoned strays, Mom, like Sonora and Tucker . . ." I stopped and waited until all the rescued animals that had enriched our lives beyond measure were pictured in her mind.

"But he's a Western horse and his name is Desperado."

She was wavering, and I could taste victory in the air. "No," I said firmly, "it's not. His name is Strawberry, and he's a jumper."

True to my word, I gave Strawberry every bit of love and care and devotion that a ten-year-old girl could lavish on the horse of her dreams. He was a quick study as he learned to be an English horse, responding to leg signals and taking small fences with reasonably good pace and form. After lessons and board, I spent every spare dollar on tack and supplies—pink, whenever possible. I couldn't believe my good fortune when I found a pink sheepskin noseband to cover his pink nylon halter and pink lead rope to match.

Only sometimes did I allow myself to see the hint of flatness, a faraway sadness, in Strawberry's eyes.

We were finally ready to compete at a small, local horse show that felt like Madison Square Garden to me. I invited everyone I knew, including the old cowboy, who showed up with a six-pack. I remember his expression of incredulity as we unloaded my red-orange chestnut horse in full pink regalia.

I entered the English equitation classes; twenty horses would perform in the arena together at the walk, trot, and canter. As we passed into the ring at a walk, I imagined a little girl sitting in the stands wishing she were me, and I sat a little taller. The judge asked for a trot, and Strawberry moved gracefully into the faster gait as I picked up his rhythm and posted. It was at the canter that I felt something start to happen. My horse's muscles began to bunch, and his ears flattened. A horse with a faster gait was coming up on the inside, and as the horse tried to pass us, Strawberry lowered his head to buck. I quickly pulled him back down into a walk and glanced to see if the judge had been watching, but she was looking at the horses on the other side of the arena. We resumed the canter, and I was ready after that. Every time a horse approached from the rear, I made a big circle to the left to come up behind the other horse.

As the class moved on to the final part of the test, I sensed another horse moving up on us. Glancing at the judge, I saw that she was looking right at Strawberry and me. Sitting up straighter than straight, picture perfect and smiling, I started my circle right in front of her. Just as we passed in front of the judge, Strawberry laid back his ears and kicked out. The judge laughed and shook her head. I fought back tears of humiliation, imagining the little girl in the stands sneering and pointing.

When all the horses were lined up for inspection, Strawberry stood quietly at attention. The judge came up to my stirrup, put her hand on the pink reins, and looked kindly at me. "He wasn't too happy out there, was he? Have you thought that maybe he would like a different kind of career?"

"No! He likes it! We just need more practice. He's a jumper. You'll see." I hoped I sounded more confident than I felt. But the jumping classes went no better.

As we loaded the trailer for the trip home, the old cowboy clanged the gate closed and said quietly, "Too bad he didn't get to show his stuff."

"What do you mean?" I shot back, stung at what I heard as criticism. "I rode well. I really tried."

He smiled at me. "You sure did, Hon. I just wish he'd had a chance at some of them Western classes, is all."

After that first show, Strawberry and I practiced every day, sometimes with other horses in the ring. He grew obedient and quiet, and I felt that we were making progress, even though the flat, distant look rarely left his eyes.

One day for a treat we went on a trail ride, his favorite thing. We rode along on a loose rein through the woods and across streams. Strawberry was relaxed, and I felt free and alive. As we passed the practice arena, I decided to take a few jumps to end our adventure. Strawberry began to prance and bunch up as we approached the gate. Thinking something was in the bushes, I jumped off to lead him into the ring. Suddenly he bolted and ripped the reins out of my hands, throwing his rear hooves in a huge buck. The last thing I saw was a hoof heading straight for my face.

I lost both front teeth and broke my nose and jaw. It took thirty stitches to put my mouth back together. As my mother held me in the emergency room, I defended Strawberry, "He didn't mean to do it, Mom. He didn't mean to hurt me. It wasn't his fault."

"I know," she crooned, "I know."

The horse of my dreams was named Desperado. He was a difficult horse if you didn't know him. I finally got to know him, and he showed me everything I needed to know about horses, and a lot of other things, too. He taught me about partnership, forgiveness, empathy, and understanding. He taught me that knowing how to ride is only the beginning. I chose an Indian print saddle pad that coordinated perfectly with his beautiful chestnut coat. Everything else was plain, rich, soft leather. He could do amazing things with his feet, like crossing one over another to go sideways without a single inch of forward motion. He could look a calf in the eye and know exactly what it was going to do before it knew itself. We won all the time in Western classes, when I sat quietly, deep in the saddle, and let him do what he was born to do.

—Jill Cordover

DEBY DELIVERS

My broodmare Deby and I expected our first babies just one week apart. Three weeks before our due dates in the summer of 1999, a number of women converged on my Missouri farm to attend a baby shower hosted by my neighbor: My mother flew in from North Carolina; my cousin Mary Ann, a mother of three, arrived from Connecticut; from Alabama came my best friend, Diane, and her four-year-old daughter; and my sister-in-law, Sally, and her teen-aged son came from Florida. As we prepared for the party, we had no hint of the magical experience in store for us that evening.

Late July in Missouri is like living in a bug-infested steam room. No amount of repellent or fly catchers can keep annoying insects from swarming over everyone's skin, human and animal alike. The horses stamp and shake and swish their tails in the shade, as they sweat in the stifling air. The late stage of pregnancy under these conditions is uncomfortable—for all species.

An old gelding named Smirnoff kept Deby company while she awaited the big moment. At twenty-five, he made steady, undemanding company for the mare. Deby showed no signs of nervousness, even when her baby moved. I was worried about my own pregnancy and wondered if I would be able to handle the inevitable labor and delivery. Deby set a good example for me with her sweet eyes and accepting disposition. I loved to feel my baby stretch and kick just under my ribs. Often I'd rest my big belly against Deby's and let our babies "talk." As I scratched the stretched skin of her flanks, knowing the relief it provided, I marveled at her calm. Even though it was her first time as well, this whole having-a-baby-thing was nothing for Deby to fret about.

That afternoon, before the party, Diane helped me give Deby a cooling bath. The mare was close to labor, even if she wasn't officially due for a couple of weeks. I'd spoken to the vet, studied my books, and knew she exhibited the symptoms: Her bag was full, her nipples waxed, and the muscles on either side of her tail had softened. I thought she might deliver that night.

Later I went inside to indulge in my own cooling shower. When Sally went to her car for a change of clothes, she heard an unmistakable sound coming from the barn. After checking the barn, she burst into the house.

"Deby's having her baby!" She pounded on the bathroom door. "Right now!"

I jumped into my maternity overalls, slipped on my plastic clogs, tied my wet hair back, and rushed to the barn. Sure enough, Deby lay on her side in her big stall. The baby's feet and head were already out, still encased in the gleaming amniotic sac. Smirnoff stood off to one side, looking concerned. I moved him out and spread a couple bales of straw in Deby's stall, jumping over her straining legs as I worked as quietly as I could. I spoke to her as I went. "It's okay, girl. You're okay." I wrapped her tail and looked for what else needed to be done.

By now everyone was in the barn, peering at the laboring mare and talking excitedly. My stepfather, Ken, had his video camera rolling. The other horses whuffled gentle encouragement. The bustle and noise did not seem to ruffle the mare in the least, concentrating as she was on the matter at hand.

I got Deby bedded to my satisfaction, relaying orders to the others to remove the water bucket and close the outside stall door. My nephew hung all the remaining fly tapes.

"Will you look at that," said Ken from behind the camera as the foal's neck emerged. None of us had ever witnessed a foal's birth before.

"I saw the baby in a plastic bag," announced four-year-old Kristina, making everyone laugh.

I retrieved my veterinary book and checklist and sat on a hay bale just outside the stall. All appeared to be proceeding as it should. The baby had presented correctly. The shoulders would be the most difficult part of the delivery, and they were next. I watched in fascination as nature took its course, hoping that I would do as well when my turn came. The other onlookers, none of them horse people except for Diane, had questions about helping.

"No, she knows what to do," I assured them. "There's no reason to interfere unless there's a problem." Silently I prayed there would be no problems.

Deby's labored breathing was the only sound in the barn. The other horses stayed close, ears pricked toward the broodmare stall. They didn't stamp their feet, but stood quietly. Our black Labrador sat near as well, occasionally whimpering with anxiety.

In the stillness, I grew aware of the focused concentration of all the mothers around me.

"C'mon, Deby," Mary Ann murmured. "Breathe."

"That's it, that's it," whispered my mom.

"Just a little more," Diane said.

"You can do it, girl," Sally added.

Then, as Deby tensed with a huge contraction, they all spoke in unison, "Push!"

The shoulders of a good-sized foal gushed out. Now I could remove the sac from its nostrils. I peeled away the slick membrane to reveal a beautiful chestnut face with a broad, white blaze. The new baby, still half inside its mom, blinked at us, and took a first breath of air.

"Good girl," I said to Deby. "Rest a bit now." I rubbed her ears and swept away the persistent flies, then swiped at the tears in my own eyes. I noted I was not the only one so moved.

"We're going to be late for the party," my husband spoke up with gentle humor, but no one suggested we leave. No one complained of the heat or the flies or standing still for however long it took to usher this new life into being. Our neighbors bred cattle; I suspected they would understand.

In only twenty minutes, Deby delivered a large and healthy colt that was admired as much as any newborn could be. Again, my guests offered motherly reassurance.

"Time to get up, little guy."

"Ooh, ooh, he's almost there."

Then, as he fell back in a tangle of spindly legs, "Whoops! Try again."

Deby got up as well, and she spoke softly to her baby, licked him dry, and nudged him with her nose until he found his way to her leaking bag. I saw the faces of my family and friends enraptured, smiling with delight, their eyes sparkling with wonder at this amazing new life.

The weather broke shortly thereafter and a refreshing downpour swept through. Outside in the reinvigorated air, a rainbow arced over the farm. Even the sky smiled. As my sister-in-law told me later, sharing the unexpected gift of that birth had a profound impact on all of us. For Sally, having recently lost her mother, it had infused her heart with new hope for the future. We mothers were bound together by this experience in a way that none of us had been before.

After watching Deby's delivery, I approached my own with as much confidence, if not with as big an audience. And I heard those women soothing and encouraging me.

"C'mon, breathe."

"That's it, that's it."

"Just a little more."

"You can do it, girl."

And I did.

—Candace Carrabus

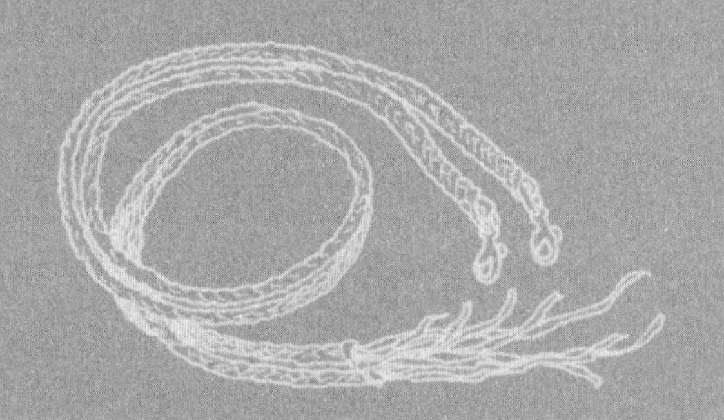

We Are Not Afraid of the Horse

There were two guiding principles of my college life: (1) Never sign on for an 8 A.M. class, and (2) Avoid at all costs donning the regulation bloomer-bottomed gym suit. Of the two, the first was the easier to follow, even if it meant switching one's major from time to time. With two years of physical education required at the New Jersey College for Women, where I was a student from 1948 to 1952, avoiding the gym suit was by far the more difficult challenge.

I studied the course catalog. Swimming? Yes! No bloomers there, just a tank suit and bathing cap. Alas, all swimming classes were filled before I could register.

Horseback riding? Jodhpurs required. I'd gladly dip into my book money to purchase them—jodhpurs meant no bloomers. I found a pair of brown ones in a rough cotton weave, slightly itchy, but cheap, and a good match for the tan corduroy jacket I already owned. I bought a pair of dark brown sturdy oxfords with matching socks to wear with the jodhpurs and considered myself ready for the equestrian life.

At my first class I was taken aback: I expected the horses to be big, but not *that* big! One by one, the stable hand, Gus, led them out, until each of us had a mount. My horse was enormous, ugly, dapple-gray, and seemed to have Attention Deficit Disorder. His name was Popover, which would turn out to be prophetic.

Gus proceeded to demonstrate the proper way to mount a horse. Stand at the horse's shoulder, face his rear, place the foot closest to the horse into the stirrup, and hoist oneself into the saddle. Gus performed this feat in one quick motion. He made it look easy.

Then it was our turn. I stretched my foot up from the hip as far as it would go, balancing tremulously on the tiptoe of the other foot. No matter, I could not reach the stirrup.

Popover was getting restless. He began to move about, leaving me to dance backward on one foot while trying desperately to capture the now wildly swaying stirrup with my equally wildly swaying other foot. Everyone else was mounted, waiting. This was embarrassing. Popover must have felt it too. He butted his nose into my back as if to say, *Get on with it.* I turned my head to face him. His mouth was opened. His teeth were big. I moved quickly out of reach.

Gus approached, a disgusted look on his face, and a stepstool in one hand. He plunked it down beside Popover. Eagerly, I stepped up on it to try again. I got my foot in the stirrup. I needed only to swing my other leg over his broad back . . . Popover decided to take another walk. I couldn't dance after him because I would fall off the stepstool. Gus grabbed the reins and Popover stood still. With his free hand, Gus gave my rump a mighty heave-ho and at last I was aboard.

I discovered with horror that my English saddle had no pommel to grip, like the saddles I'd seen in all those Western movies. The stirrups looked pretty flimsy, too, but I needn't have worried about those, because next we met Frau Schlect.

Frau Schlect was our instructor. There was something about her black riding outfit and clipped German accent that said, *You will obey.* In one hand, she held a whip. I hoped it was for the horses. Frau Schlect did not believe in stirrups. They were for show, not for staying on the horse.

"For staying on the horse, you grip with your knees," Frau Schlect informed us. "Take those feet out of the stirrups."

I was beginning to feel very shaky.

Frau Schlect said, "You must relax in the saddle. That way the horse knows who is boss."

Horses sense nervousness and will take advantage of it, we were told. If we exuded confidence, the horse would know we were in charge and obey. I realized this was true. Popover certainly knew who was in charge when Gus was around. He also knew who was in charge without Gus. It wasn't me.

Frau Schlect said we would do exercises before riding out. First, we were to lean back until our heads rested on the horse's rump—a nice, long stretch. No reins, no stirrups, just gripping with my knees while trying to find Popover's spine with the back of my head. It did not feel relaxing to me; it felt scary.

"We are not afraid of the horse," Frau Schlect announced.

We were now going to show the horse we were not afraid by doing a 360-degree turn in the saddle. We would swing a leg over to sit sideways, then again to face the rear of the horse, around to the other side, and then face front again. In my haste to complete this maneuver, I may have kicked Popover, or perhaps he was just bored, because halfway through my turning he decided to take a walk, ambling off with me facing his swaying rump.

"Return with that horse!" ordered Frau Schlect, as if I could.

Popover may have had previous experience with Frau Schlect, or he too may have noticed the whip, but he mercifully decided to return to his place. As soon as he stopped moving, I swung around to face front again. *Calisthenics finished, the worst over,* I thought with relief. My relief was short lived.

"We will begin with the trot," snapped Frau Schlect.

Gus demonstrated, raising and lowering his torso in unison with the horse's gait as he trotted past.

"You will stand in the saddle," said Frau Schlect.

With rising panic, I saw at once the circus parade picture in my second-grade reader, complete with elephants, caged lions, and a smiling ballerina, arms extended over her pink tutu, *en pointe* on the back of a prancing white steed. I wasn't going to do that. I was not getting up out of my seat to stand on my toes on the saddle. Gym bloomers began to look pretty good to me.

Frau Schlect cracked her whip at the first horse and off it went, my classmate's jodhpur-clad bottom raising and lowering as she trotted off. Another crack of the whip, then another, and one by one my classmates trotted out, their knees gripping their horses, their bodies moving up and down with varying degrees of competence. They weren't standing on top of the saddle on their toes; they were posting like Gus had done. Of course! I laughed internally at my foolish fears.

Crack! The whip was practically in Popover's face. He trotted after the others. I posted with all my strength, my thighs and knees burning, but my heart light. I felt good.

We trotted single file in a circle around Frau Schlect. Round and round we went, as she snapped her whip and barked corrections. Soon, Popover lost interest and trotted out of the circle to head for a patch of dry grass by the edge of the corral. There he stopped, lowered his head, and began to graze.

"Return with that horse!" Frau Schlect bellowed.

This time, Popover didn't listen. He was enjoying his snack. Frau Schlect appeared.

"Show that horse who is boss," she ordered.

How silly. I didn't have to show him, he knew. But I didn't tell Frau Schlect that.

"Shorten the reins," she instructed. "Wind them around your hands. Move up his neck. Keep winding them! Keep winding them!"

I found myself creeping slowly down Popover's outstretched neck, shortening the reins, and getting closer and closer to his head. He continued his munching, oblivious to me. I was beginning to feel in control.

"When you get close to the mouth, to the end of the reins, jerk them, pull up quick and hard. He will learn who is boss," Frau Schlect's clipped words exuded authority.

I was almost there . . . almost. By now, my seat was out of the saddle and my arms were stretched clear down his neck when Popover decided to jerk first. Tightly reined to the bit in his mouth, I flew forward off his neck and onto the ground in front of him. I sat where I had fallen, stunned, and Popover went on eating.

"You are holding up my class. Get back on that horse." I saw the whip move ever so slightly in Frau Schlect's hand. Was it for Popover or for me?

I got back on that horse. I didn't even need the stepstool. I gave the reins a yank. Popover understood. He trotted back into line.

—MARCIA RUDOFF

The Flint Hills

The raw sienna view rolls on, growing more intimidating with each mile. It is the kind of land that divides bravado from courage, dreams from determination. We three women have heard tales of whole herds of cattle being lost out here, and we see bleached bones as we drive up the rutted dirt road that leads from the highway.

We are here because we love to gallop horses across open land. This love led us to the sport of fox hunting, although today we will be chasing coyotes. I picture a lone coyote, his head tilted toward the sky, and think I hear his plaintive cry. Usually willing to brave just about any kind of weather for a chance to feel one with my horse, the hounds, the land, and these two friends, today—for the first time in a long while—I question my ability to play with the big boys.

I look at my friends, mavericks of sorts. We've all chosen horses and this rugged sport over shopping, ladies clubs, and manicures. The hunt has a traditional male hierarchy, yet we women are the ones who clean the hound kennels, clear the trails, and show up to help the club's professional huntsman realize a dream. Through hard work we have carved out our niche in this sport—banded together, egged each other on, and made this riding club as much ours as that of our male counterparts. I hope that, today, the men will treat us as equals.

We park in the middle of a cattle range. The wind hisses and roars around the truck as we sit snugly inside and contemplate what the icy winter day might hold.

I have to give the men credit. Not one has questioned our right to be here, yet. Still, the day is far from over, and I will not be surprised if one of them knocks on the window and asks if we need help saddling up. I grudgingly admit to myself that if he did, I wouldn't turn him down. It's cold out there. I blow into my cupped hands.

I wonder why am I am so sensitive today and realize it is the specter of my own insecurity. I question my capabilities and worry whether or not I am up to the Wild West, for that is what this is. Rock lies hidden just below the deceptively soft, pale ochre grass. Deep crevices wait like open mouths ready to snap a horse's leg and catapult the rider against the hard, frozen ground.

No building mars the landscape; no power lines connect us to civilization. Only a few small stands of Osage trees mark sources of water and shelter from the constant gale. The land is untamed, unyielding. Maybe it is the one place that is truly a man's world.

The hills, cruel in their starkness, yet beautiful, make me feel small and unimportant. I glance at my friends, and see similar feelings flit across their faces. Our love for horses and the English sport we have claimed as our own is shaken in the vastness of these raw western plains. At the lonely cry of the coyote, I shudder and search the terrain, seeing nothing except gray sky. I understand the coyote's song. In this vast land, a call for help might well go unheard, or if heard, unfound. One must find the strength within oneself to survive; it's enough to make anyone cry.

I turn to my friends. A smile of anticipation and nervousness trembles on my lips. I look out the window and almost expect to see a cowboy or Indian appear on the horizon and tell us to go home.

"Time to saddle up," I say and pull my muffler over my ears as I open the passenger door. My two companions climb out behind me, and we unload our horses. The horses skitter about, restless after their long trailer ride. They flare their nostrils. Ears at attention, they take in the vast territory with wide, rolling eyes. I murmur soothing words; I'm not sure if they are for the horses or for myself.

We throw on the English tack, pull on our tall black boots, and don our velvet-covered hardhats and black wool hunting jackets. I breathe in the rich scent of my horse's chestnut coat, gather strength, and feel the excitement building within me. I can do this.

We check off our assigned items, the things we carry in case of an emergency. Women think about emergencies, and more than once we have offered up some of our supplies to help a fellow in need. We are ready to ride.

Our huntsman chuckles at our full pockets and serious faces and blows his hunting horn. Hounds spill across the landscape. We three queue up at the rear of a short line of hardy male hunters, I on my Thoroughbred and my friends on their quarter horses.

A fox hunt depends on long-standing traditions, and even though we are chasing coyotes and this is the twenty-first century, tradition says the newer members ride behind the more senior members. That means today the men are in front, and we follow behind. In front of the field of men and we three women rides the huntsman—the man who trains and controls the foxhounds. The hounds lead the way.

As I ride, I imagine the pioneers who crossed this vast land. It is as if I have galloped back in time to join them.

"Ya, ya, ya, ya, ya," the huntsman yells as the hounds burst into action and move through the tall, dry bluestem grass, filling the air with their voices. The sound ripples up and down my spine. The huntsman blows "Gone Away" on his horn, a sign to the field that the hounds are hot on the scent of a coyote.

The horses thunder across the plain and the muscles along their shoulders and haunches bulge and relax with each massive stride. After a while, the white foam of exertion lathers their necks and feels like slick soap as it slips between gloves and reins. Men begin to drop back, signal us to go ahead. An hour into a hard run, we slow down and take time to look around. We three women and the huntsman are the only people in sight.

One friend turns to me and pumps the air with her fist. I barely have time to give her a thumbs-up before we are off again.

We ride for hours. Walk—the feeling, a slow massage to my tired limbs; trot—an invigorating four-beat march; gallop—an adrenaline high; and still the land rolls on before us. The horses snort and blow. We're excited, breathless from the long chase. We've stayed in the hunt.

The huntsman begins to call the pack in. We help gather the tired hounds, and they rest with little persuasion. I weave my way carefully between deep ravines, along narrow puddles flanked by wind-stunted trees. My eyes devour these respites from the vast rolling hills like a desert traveler gulps water at an oasis.

Clouds hide the sun, and I am no longer sure where we are. My friends shrug, their expressions blank except for the telling furrows etched across their brows. "In the Flint Hills," one whispers after a long silence. My other friend lets out a weak chuckle.

The huntsman pivots and looks puzzled. He peers at the sky, sniffs the frigid air. He pivots again, and we circle with him. The land appears the same no matter which way we turn.

"There's no sun. Can't read the direction. Storm coming. We're lost." The huntsman is a man of few words, and this is a speech for him. He frowns, and his eyes narrow with worry.

We know this harsh land can be dangerous. My pulse quickens. I think of all the people who have died while traversing this unsettled heart of our country. Then I think of the first women, pioneers and Native Americans, who crossed the West. They were tough, self-reliant. They carried on. The men didn't settle the West alone. They needed women, I realize, to shoulder part of the load. The same is true today. Now here we are, three women who have followed their hearts and one man, lost in the Flint Hills of Kansas. It is our turn to be put to the test.

Which way to the trailers? What can we do? I look at my friends. We communicate without speaking. One pulls out a small bag of chocolates and passes it around, and the other offers liquid from the silver flask she carries in her pocket. Fortified by the nourishment, I tell the huntsman, "I have a compass."

We sit in the truck, tired, headed back toward Kansas City. I sigh with satisfaction and notice that the worry lines have vanished from my friends' faces and have been replaced by an aura of confidence. We have ventured into the Flint Hills and proved ourselves worthy.

"I'll never forget the looks on the men's faces when we got back to the trailers," I say. "They actually cheered." I rub fog off the side window and look at the coming darkness. "What I liked best was the way they treated us. Didn't even offer to untack our horses." My friends grin.

I gaze out at the vastness and say a silent thank you to my horse that carried me safely throughout the day. I am the same person I was this morning, yet changed by my experience in this stark land. Never again will I question my right to try something or worry over whether I belong. Strengthened by this affirmation of my worth, I find myself eager to test this newly discovered grit.

The Flint Hills. I finger the flat, sharp stone I have taken as a souvenir and realize I do not need it, for a small piece of the Wild West called courage and determination gallops in my heart. I open the window and fling it out, watching as it disappears in the tall, blue-stemmed grass.

I look toward the horizon. The view rolls on in undulating shades of sienna and possibilities, and I listen to my horse's gentle nicker as a coyote's sonorous cry bids me farewell.

—Deborah K. Bundy

The Horse Nobody Wanted

The phone rang incessantly as I came into the house.

"Hello?"

"I'm calling about Bendito." It was Bob Nelson at Rolling Hills Stables.

"Hey, how about that horse," I said. "He made quite a splash on the show circuit last year."

"Ah, yeah," he paused. "Do you know anyone who might want to buy him?"

"Not for the kind of money he's worth."

"I'm afraid he's not worth much any more," Bob didn't sound happy. "If I don't get him out of here soon, he's going to be shipped to the auction."

I listened, stunned, as Bob told me the story of the rangy, long-legged gelding I'd raised from a colt. Bendito had lots of natural talent, and when we showed him he usually won. I hadn't had the money or the time to campaign him on the national circuit, so we had sold him and sent him to Bob's stable for training. After a year, when Ben was four points away from his Legion of Merit, he was about to be sold again, but the vet wouldn't certify him as sound.

The buyer had backed out, and now Bob had a lame horse on his hands.

"I guess the heavy campaigning strained his legs," I barely heard Bob continue. "The vet says he'd probably be okay for light riding, but no more heavy competition. He's out to pasture, so at least he's not running up board bills, but the other day he ran the stable owner's horse into a fence. I'm afraid if I don't get him out of here, Mr. Runsted will ship Ben to the auction."

"I'll try to think of something." I sat at the kitchen table nursing a cup of coffee. Who would pay good money for a lame show gelding? If Ben went to auction, he'd end up as pet food. A national champion had suddenly become the horse nobody wanted.

I decided not to let that happen; I would bring him home. But where would I put him? We had a small barn with four stalls and seven horses; Ben would make eight. I needed those stalls for mares and foals. And evidently Ben could still cause mayhem in the pasture. Maybe we'd have to build the addition to the barn sooner than we'd planned.

As I stared out the window trying to visualize where a new barn addition might go, a blue pickup rumbled up the drive. Sue—my long-time friend and a fellow horse enthusiast—climbed out.

"I came over to see the new foals. . . What's the matter?"

My sigh would have done a soap opera star proud. "Do you know anyone who would take an eleven-year-old national champion gelding who's lame and has a stack of bills hanging over his head?"

Sue was incredulous. "Bendito?"

I nodded and told her the story.

"I might be interested," said Sue after a long pause.

I stared at her.

She continued, "If Ben can be ridden and the price is right, he might make a good horse for Janie to learn saddle-seat. I have trail horses and brood mares, but nothing suitable for English riding."

My spirits picked up. Maybe I wouldn't have to build that barn addition after all. "I'm going over to Rolling Hills to pick up Starlight," I said. "Why don't you come along? If you decide you want Ben, we could get him out of there today."

An hour later we were sitting in Bob's office. "The vet has okayed Ben for light riding," he told Sue. "He's not a beginner's horse, but if your daughter can ride, he'd be an excellent teacher. He knows it all."

"How much?" Sue ventured.

"If it were up to me, I'd give him to you, but there's about $2,500 in unpaid bills."

Disappointment clouded Sue's face. Bob reached for the phone and dialed a number, "Hello, Mr. Runsted? Bob here. I have someone here willing to take Bendito off your hands."

Bob doodled on a sheet of notepaper as he listened. "Bendito," he repeated, "the white gelding in the pasture? The one who sent your mare through the fence."

A high-stepping horse appeared in Bob's scribbles as he said, "Well, yes, there are bills outstanding, but there's no market for a lame eleven-year-old gelding. At least he'd be off the place." The silence hung heavy as Bob turned the paper over and doodled on the back. "No, Bendito won't bring much at auction. He'd be sold by the pound, and he's just a little horse, barely fourteen hands. Weighs seven-, eight-hundred pounds, max."

I nearly swallowed my gum. Was he talking about the same Bendito?

"I'll give you a hundred for him," Sue blurted.

"Mr. Runsted, I have a lady here who will take him for a hundred dollars."

A string of 1-0-0, followed by dollar signs appeared on Bob's scribble sheet. "OK, I'll tell her." He hung up the phone with a satisfied smile. "Looks like you just bought yourself a hundred-dollar horse." With trembling hands, Sue filled out the check.

"Bendito hasn't been fourteen hands and seven hundred pounds since he was a yearling," I said to Bob.

He grinned, "Yeah, I know. I may have underestimated his size a bit." He turned to Sue, and explained that Mr. Runsted would be coming by, so it would be a good idea if Ben weren't around when he got there.

Outside, we watched one of the grooms bring in Ben from the pasture. I hardly recognized him now. I remembered a lanky gray always dancing at the end of his lead rope like a debutant going to a party. Age had turned Ben's coat white and his walk sedate. The remnants of winter fur still clung to him and whiskers hung under his chin, obscuring the shape of his head. His mane was rough and tangled, his tail no longer the glorious plume that had once hung nearly to the ground. I looked at his feet. Apparently the farrier hadn't been paid either. A round hay belly and dimples on his rump told me that Ben hadn't gone hungry, but he did look like $100 was about the right price for him.

With Starlight and Ben loaded, Sue and I headed back down the gravel road. A big white Cadillac passed us in a cloud of dust and swung into the stable parking lot. We had gotten Ben out of there just in time.

As I turned onto the blacktop, Sue confessed, "I can't take Ben home. Jim will throw a fit if I bring in another horse."

I knew Jim. Like most husbands with horse-crazy wives, he usually tolerated Sue's impulses. Evidently, she knew that this time she had stepped over the line. I stopped the truck. "What were you planning to do? Keep Ben in the trailer for the rest of his life?"

"I was hoping you could keep him at your place for a while," she said a tad sheepishly. "I'll bring over the feed and stuff," she hurried on, "I know your barn is full, but it won't be for long. Just until I can get squared away with Jim." I sighed and headed for home.

As promised, Sue came faithfully, lugging feed and bedding for her new purchase. She sent the farrier over to trim Ben's feet, and she and I clipped Ben's fur and brushed out the tangled mane and tail until he began to look like a respectable horse again. Afterward we shared coffee and horse stories at the kitchen table.

A month later Sue announced, "I think I can bring Ben home now."

"Jim have a change of heart?"

"Not exactly. He heard through the grapevine that I bought a white horse and was hiding it somewhere. He's been calling every stable in the area, asking if they sold a white horse recently. One stable told him they'd just sold one for $12,000." Sue smiled, "If Jim thinks I bought a $12,000 horse, he won't say a word when I show up with Ben. He'll just figure he's $11,900 ahead."

Later that same day, we hauled Ben over to Sue's place, where the horse that nobody wanted stayed for seventeen years.

—Jacklyn Lee Lindstrom

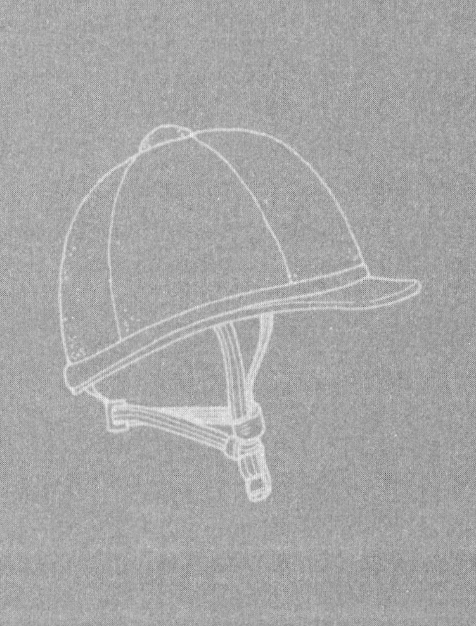

Mucho Muchacho

My appaloosa mare, Poteet, is due any day now, and I spend most of my evenings in the barn watching for the signs—no appetite, leaky nipples. Two weeks before my thirteenth birthday, I notice milk dripping down her hind legs. Wild with excitement, I rush up to the house and call my parents to come and see. Poteet seems to be happy as well. She takes a bit of water in her mouth and spits it out over her salt block, which she licks with great gusto. She takes a nip of hay and strews it over my lap, flapping her lips to retrieve a single blade with every sign of enjoyment. All the time, she's watching us, wondering why there are so many people in her stable. My parents laugh, "She's having a ball."

I go up to the house to collect a sleeping bag and my book, returning to the barn within half an hour. But I am too late—there's a white blaze on the floor, and it doesn't belong to Poteet. I sit there for the next few hours. Sometimes I pretend to read but I never get to the next page. I watch as the foal looks everywhere for its mother's nipple; it goes into the corner and makes loud sucking noises at the spider webs. It comes over to me and sucks at my book. Delight chokes me. Poteet doesn't help much.

She's licking and sniffing so hard the foal almost falls over, which is alarming because it took so long for him to get up in the first place, his long, spindly legs flopping about on the floor.

We call the foal Muchacho, which means "little boy" in Spanish. I settle into a routine. As soon as I get home from school, I rush to my horses, and then stay with them until dark. First I give them grain, and while they're eating I fill up their water buckets and hay nets. Then I sit on a bit of hay and sing Leonard Cohen songs. When the horses finish their own grain, they rush to each other's pails where they lick every crevice of a completely empty bucket. Then they start on the hay, choosing stalks from under my bum even though there's plenty in the hay nets. Muchacho practically pushes me over with his nose, chewing his hard-won cud in my face as I sing. Sometimes he pretends to mistake my hair for hay, and I return to the house with my hair matted with saliva gobs.

Once they've eaten their fill, they prepare to go to sleep. Muchacho lies down in the sawdust, turning around like a cat but with considerably less grace. Poteet is less trusting. She stands resolutely, her head dropping lower and lower as she falls asleep. Once her mouth is resting on the ground, her front legs begin to buckle. She'll stumble and jerk awake to start the whole process again. Her mouth gets mashed against the ground and takes most of her weight when her legs give out. It's really funny, and sometimes my singing dissolves into laughter.

When I go out riding, Muchacho tags along behind his mother. He sticks fairly close, but then starts to wander away. At first I worry about him, but he always charges back unexpectedly, skidding to a stop seconds before a collision. Poteet never gets used to his disappearing acts and whinnies anxiously all the time. I figure she knows he'll come back at some point, but she's just the tense type. I hope I won't be a mother like that.

On weekends I tie Poteet outside the field so she can eat her fill; I worry there's not enough grass for two horses in the field. Muchacho wanders around free, and I check on him out the window every now and then. Sometimes his long face grins back at me.

A neighbor drops in to visit and tells Mum how much she enjoys Muchacho's daily visits. I think she's exaggerating, because I only let them out on weekends, but I have no doubt he visits whenever he gets the chance—perhaps more often than planned.

We have a rundown fence around the horses' field that needs constant fixing. As soon as I am old enough, Dad fobs the job onto me, teaching me how to do everything except cut down the tree to make the post.

Muchacho lets us know when a post falls down. I come out of the house, and he races up the driveway to greet me, although he's not supposed to be out. Poteet stands anxiously by the gate, holding one foot in the air like she does when she's waiting for her food. I try to find where Muchacho pushed his way through the fence. He walks sedately by my side like a dog at heel, hiding any signs of excitement as we pass the guilty post. Often the post is still standing—maybe it's not as straight as it should be but most of the posts are leaning at crazy angles—so I can't find it. So I have to go back to the house and watch from a window. Like a criminal drawn to the scene of the crime, Muchacho can't resist going back to the post. He pretends to graze, lifting up his head every now and then to see if he can catch me sneaking up on him.

Finally, he can resist no longer; he sidles back to the broken post, leans on it until the wires are almost flat against the ground, and steps out to freedom. I march out with my hammer and spade and dig my hole. Muchacho puts his nose into everything, inspecting the hole just when I want to heave in a big rock, or studying the new post while I try to nail the wires. After I return to the house, he checks out my handiwork, leaning with all his weight first on one side of the new post, and then the other. He only gives up when he's convinced he can't escape.

When Muchacho turns three, I start training him. I don't have a clue how to do it, so I memorize the one book I have that goes through every step of training a young horse. I start with the lunging chapter. It says you get the horse used to voice commands with the help of a whip. For example, if you want the horse to trot you say, "Trot" and wave the whip at the same time. The horse then breaks into a trot, eventually responding to the voice command alone. Sounds straightforward.

Muchacho doesn't see the point of running in circles. I wave the whip at him, and he careens around like a bronco. I pull sharply on the lead to stop him, and he veers toward me, skidding to a stop inches away from my nose. I prod him back to the outer perimeter of the circle and try again.

"Walk on," I say clearly. Muchacho tries to come to the middle of the circle for another visit. I warn him away with a wave of the whip, and he ignores it. I poke him in the chest as he comes nearer, and he tries to grab the whip with his teeth. I lose patience and give him a sharp crack on his ample rump. He leaps away and starts to gallop around. This time I don't pull on the lead, so he has no excuse to veer in my direction again. Muchacho gallops in smaller and smaller circles until he's back to where he wants to be—in the middle with me.

The book has all kinds of information about handling the first ride. I am prepared for any reaction, from fear to bucking. Muchacho acts like I've been on his back ever since he was born. He continues eating grass. When I pull his head up, he turns around and nibbles my shoe.

Progress is quick once I stop trying to force him to run in circles. He loves going on the trails and learns to change gaits according to my commands. By the middle of the summer, I have a horse who can walk, trot, and canter with the best of them. I am very proud of myself.

Once I can ride Muchacho, we go on long treks together. Parents often come up to me so their kids can give him a pat, even though they are wary of his size. They ask if he's gentle, and I say yes, but Muchacho doesn't receive attention passively. He's a very give-and-take kind of fellow.

One day we are riding down the street when a car screeches to a halt just opposite us: tourists. The parents get out and ask if their kid can pat Muchacho. "Sure," I say sweetly, assuring them he doesn't bite. They hold their tiny child up to Muchacho's nose. I'm surprised the boy is old enough to focus. He shows no interest in petting a horse and instead concentrates on the huge sucker he's holding. I look at the sucker in amazement, and Muchacho seems to be fascinated with the sucker as well. In the next instant, Muchacho's mouth engulfs the kid's arm, right up to the armpit. The smiles freeze on the parents' faces. Slowly, the arm reappears inch by inch, coated in a rich foam of saliva. The tiny fingers appear last, whole and rosy—minus the sucker.

Muchacho munches happily, and the parents run back to their car. The kid realizes his sucker is missing and starts to bawl. Dissolving into laughter, I jump off Muchacho's back and kiss his face. It's impossible to get cross with him. The glint in his eye is too mischievous. Muchacho takes my caresses docilely and continues to munch. I check the ground to see if he's let any pieces fall out—it was an enormous sucker, and I wouldn't mind a piece of it myself—but he has been very thorough.

Poteet is waiting for us with her neurotic foot in the air. Muchacho inhales her breath and squeals absurdly. If only I could capture and bottle the joy he brings me, I would share it with others. Now, at least I can write about it.

–Charlotte Mendel

Sandy Hears the Call

Sandy introduced herself to the group as a minister of a nondenominational church in the city. One could see that Sandy knew herself well. She had a calm, centered presence and carried herself with ease and confidence. At the same time, the other women in the group could feel the care and support she proffered. Sandy had only recently been called to horses. She didn't own a horse or even ride. She wasn't sure why she had felt compelled to come to this equine-guided program on a warm fall weekend. Sandy had a feeling that the horses would help her learn something about herself. She couldn't explain it, yet she sat in the circle, ready to find the answers to an unknown *something* that was burning inside her.

Sandy sensed that her original passion for her work had gotten lost. As she negotiated the construction of a new facility, she felt herself sundered by the internal dynamics of the church. Her traditional workhorse mentality—throw yourself into your work, do what must be done—left her feeling isolated. Her sense of responsibility to the staff and church members prevented her from telling anyone she was feeling dull and burned out. She didn't even tell this to the women gathered in a circle around her as, one by one, each shared her own story of self-discovery, unexpressed fears, and secret desires. It didn't occur to Sandy to mention it. Her job was to "hold things together." Or at least she thought it was.

After hours of trying to explain to the other women why she was at this program, it was Sandy's turn to enter the round pen to share her story, goals, and desires with Lily, a six-year-old quarter horse. Lily pricked her ears forward as Sandy walked through the gate. Sandy had seen how the mare engaged with the other women as each had spoken of what she cared about, and what had meaning for her. As each woman walked in the pen, toward the life of her choosing, Lily responded. Sometimes the horse walked next to the woman, sometimes behind, and by doing so, Lily indicated that the woman was in touch with her passion.

Sandy sighed heavily as she began to speak. She told Lily about goals she "should" focus on, such as her commitment to create a new church that was bigger and brighter and could sustain the membership for a long time to come. Lily walked away. The women outside the round space didn't understand this.

Sandy faced Lily and asked her to walk with her. Lily stood still, as if rooted to the earth. Sandy understood. "I'm stuck," she said to the group. "Lily is being me. I don't want to be responsible for the construction of a new church."

An elder woman in the group said, "Forget about building a new church for a moment. What do you care about? What has life and meaning to you now?"

"I don't know," said Sandy. She looked up at the sky as if looking for a clue. Perhaps deep inside she did know, but the truth that coursed through her body hadn't risen to consciousness.

Just then, all the horses around the barn began to whinny: Morgan from her stall, Cowgirl in the south field, Billy from the west, and the nine horses in the field next to the round pen. They sang a crescendo of whinnies. As the equine chorus resonated through the timbers of the barn and sent the pigeons flying, Sandy realized that the narrow categories of denomination, color, and creed were far too limiting for her now. Something greater was calling to her imagination.

All the women in the group watched in rapt attention. No one could deny this unique event. Everyone had been introduced to the idea that horses listen to your inner longing, desires, and beliefs. Horses are unique mirrors of your inner voice, not whom you think you are or whom you think you "should" be. Horses reflect that inner calling that sends us forth into the world, sometimes on paths previously unknown to us. Some of the women in the group that day thought that any link between horse and guidance was just coincidence. Others had seen hundreds of different people interact with these intuitive equine guides. While it was impossible to explain what had just happened, the women knew that what they witnessed was a unique expression of Sandy.

The nine horses in the field approached the north end of the round pen and lined up facing Sandy, their ears pricked forward, heads raised, bodies touching. Superman stood in front, flanked by the others. All the women gasped. Sandy turned to the horses, "What do you want from me?"

Superman spoke to her, *We do not want anything from you. We are here to support you. We hear the same call as you.* Sandy stood in silence, knowing inside that something profound had just happened. Did she really hear what she had just heard? Did a horse just speak to her? "I dare not tell anybody, they wouldn't understand," she thought to herself. She felt the afternoon breeze on her face and the soft sand under her feet and remained silent.

"Perhaps they are responding to something deep inside you, calling you forward," one woman said. Another added, "It doesn't look to me like they want something from you. It looks like they are acknowledging you in a very powerful way."

The first day ended in silent reflection. Sandy sat quietly at the south end of the barn. How was she going to give voice to what she felt inside? Her body knew that she was done with her church. Somewhere hidden in her heart, she knew something larger was calling her, asking her to listen, asking her to believe.

Each time Sandy interacted with the horses over the next two days, a chorus rang loud and long through the barn, the arena, and the round space. Morgan, Billy, Cowgirl, and the other nine horses called each other in an ancient voice, unified into one energetic field. Even the nonbelievers now understood that the horses were communicating something that the humans did not quite understand, at least not yet. Even Emma, the skeptical clinician, was deeply touched. "I've never seen anything like it," she said.

Sandy felt stunned and exposed. Her words to the women tumbled out, "I know that I'm being called by something, but I never imagined that horses could see inside me so clearly. Now I know why I was called to come here, to this land, to these horses, at this time and place. I needed fresh ears and eyes to help me expand my spirituality. I'm tired of the nitpicking among different religious beliefs. I'm tired of the squabbles among the different denominations. I want to spend my time thinking beyond the past."

She hurried on as if making up for lost time, "So much of my work is about inspiring people to follow their hearts. Part of me knows that it is not the best use of myself to stay at the church and build a new building." She took a breath. "So I guess it's time for me to listen to my own words."

The elder woman of the group spoke, "Can you share with us what your heart wants to follow now?"

"I want to open a new spiritual center. I don't know what it looks like, but I know if I take the first steps, it will become clear. I have that kind of faith."

Superman whinnied, the women laughed, and Sandy felt a weight lift off her shoulders. Her body felt soft. A playful smile blossomed on her chiseled face. It was a good day to begin.

—ARIANA STROZZI

Slender Threads

I'm not going. No way. It's too scary. Vida didn't say this in English, of course. Arab horses are smart, and they understand many words, but the language they speak is a flare of nostrils, a twitch of the ears, or the stamp of a hoof. My sorrel mare, usually gentle and willing, made her position clear by pinning her ears and refusing to budge one step. She was not about to go down the trail I'd chosen. The path was as wide as a narrow driveway, grassy except for hard-packed, shallow ruts where a truck might occasionally drive, just a few dusty steps off a paved, lightly trafficked road. Along the right, a barbed wire fence enclosed a pasture where horses or cows might graze, none visible this day. Along the left ran a line of tall fir trees, thickened here and there by a tangle of blackberries. Behind the trees, barely visible, another barbed wire fence, a house, and a garden. A wide green iron gate marked the beginning of the path, open and inviting. Beyond the gate lay a network of trails from which we could explore a lightly wooded canyon and streambed.

We had permission to use the trail, and Vida had been down it several times before, following her best friend, Lucky. On those times, she had cast a curious eye at shadows among the firs, but moved right along. The last time she'd gone down the path, a bee had stung her, causing a sudden flurry of bucks, but she'd quickly settled down. What was worrying her now? Perhaps the dense line of trees held a troubling smell or, perhaps, without the protection of Lucky, she feared an unknown creature might appear and challenge us. Maybe she expected an entire hive of bees to assault her this time. Whatever it was, she needed to find her courage.

"Come on, sweetie," I encouraged, and nudged her forward with my legs. She didn't move. I kicked with both heels. She stepped up to the gate then wheeled to the right. "Listen, Vida. You're blowing this bee thing way out of proportion." I picked up the left rein, got her facing forward again, and kicked harder. She jigged three steps backward onto the road where a car might pass any time.

Was this a power struggle? I looked along the trail and thought of the conflicting advice I'd heard for moments like this: You can't let a horse win; do whatever it takes; you have to show you are boss. Or, show your respect for the horse's feelings because horses generally do their best to please. I'd brought along a crop. I seldom use it, but that day I whacked her shoulder. She jumped in surprise—up more than forward. Then she turned her head and looked at me, the expression in her eye unmistakable: *Look, I'm doing the best I can. Beating me up isn't going to make any difference. I'm not just stubborn, you know; I'm scared to death.*

"Okay," I said, my voice quiet again, "I'll lead you." I swung off, took the reins over her head, and clasped them together close to her whiskered chin. We walked together through the gate and along several feet of the trail. I could feel her trembling.

"Come on, girl," I soothed. "You're all right. You'll see."

Four horses appeared at the ridge of the pasture beyond the barbed wire fence and galloped up to us. One carefully extended its head across the fence.

"Hello there," I said, firmly holding Vida. Then, to Vida, "See, it can't get you. It can't reach us where we are." She did not seem to be comforted as she sweated and danced in place.

I was afraid, too. The trail that frightened me was in a life far removed from kind-eyed horses, wooded hillsides, and sunlit pastures. A few days before, a routine physical had disclosed a pulse thirty beats higher than normal. A blood test to check for possible thyroid problems seriously worried my doctor. Now I had to wait three days—an eternity—for a thyroid scan. He didn't say so, but I knew he was looking for cancer.

I didn't know how I would endure those three days. Obsessive thoughts of illness and death filled my head. I had talked to friends and read everything I could about thyroid cancer on the Internet. I learned that thyroid cancer is a "good" kind of cancer, as cancer goes. It would almost certainly be self-contained, and surgery and therapy would be relatively simple. But the information did little to allay my fears. Only the slenderest of threads joined rational thought and raw emotion. Maybe Vida—all 1,000 pounds of her—was afraid of a tiny bee, but I had to respect her terror. The threads holding rational thought to her emotions were slender, too.

"You know, Vida," I said, "let's take a different approach." We walked back to the shoulder of the road where I mounted again. I took a deep breath to relax us both.

"Come on, girl." I loosened the reins and nudged her with my legs. "Just one step."

She took two steps toward the gate before she stopped. "Good job," I said, patting her neck. I sat quietly for a few seconds before I asked her to move forward again.

Two more steps, and she stopped. "Way to go, girl," I praised, stroking her. "We're between the gate posts."

The third time I picked up the reins and nudged her forward, we got through the gate, then she bent tightly to the right to avoid the barbed wire. I pulled her head around so she faced down the trail. She whipped to the left. Again I brought her head around. "Face forward, Vida," I told her. "Always forward."

She moved along nicely for a minute or two, and then stopped again. When I kicked her hard, she whirled to the right, threatening to impale us on jagged iron barbs. How like those moments when I seemed to be doing well and then my anxiety would overwhelm me once more. I let her stand for a minute more as I comforted and encouraged her before I moved her on. I, too, had friends who were doing plenty of that for me.

And so it went, foot by slow foot, refocusing, bringing her head around, and cheering her on. Testing the strength of those slenderest of threads, Vida and I learned together how concentration on the moment, a steady gaze forward, and a lot of support can ease one's way down a scary trail. And we made it.

—SAMANTHA DUCLOUX WALTZ

Never Too Young, Never Too Old

Are you ever too old for horses? Gram and I kicked around the question one afternoon while she entertained my four-year-old son, Justin. I sat nearby, addressing holiday cards decorated with a horse and snow motif. Everyone in our family is mad for horses. Our roots are deep in the horse country of western Pennsylvania.

"I'm still a horse lover," mused Gram, "even though I can't ride no more. Not with my arthritis and this bad hip." She looked down fondly at Justin, who was sitting on her knee. "I've got seventy years on your boy here, but I still remember my first pony ride."

I looked up from the envelope I was addressing. "You took me for my first pony ride, remember?"

"Sure do." A wistful look came into Gram's eyes, "That was when your mom and dad used to bring you out to the farm . . . when we still had it." She sighed. The loss of that farm was still a sore point. Grandpa's bad investments twenty years back had forced them to move to the city to be near my mom and dad. We struck down urban roots, even though our hearts were back on that country farm, now lost forever.

Gram glanced at me. "I still ride, y' know. In my dreams."

"Really?"

"I do. When I get those dreams, I'm ten years old again. I'm young and healthy and strong enough to do anything." Her eyes misted as she rubbed my son's back in a soothing motion, "Last night I was on Lucky Lady."

"Your old pinto?"

"Goin' back sixty years, can you believe it? Some memories never leave you."

Lucky Lady had been Gram's childhood horse. I'd heard the story many times back when I was a kid, and more recently when Gram regaled Justin with her treasure trove of stories.

Justin started to fuss so I handed him a blank holiday card. "Horsie!" he exclaimed as he ripped the card in half.

"Mommy had a horse like that once," I pointed at the brown stallion on the torn card. The old memory clutched at my heart. In those days my parents paid a stable to board one of Gram's remaining horses, and we would ride on weekends. Eventually it became too expensive for my parents to keep the horse, and they sold it.

My love of horses persisted, though it had been many years since I'd heaved my leg over a saddle. It would be a splendid thing, I thought, if Justin could learn about horses. Other than reading books to him or popping in a video, how could I introduce him to that exciting world?

I looked at the rustic scene on the holiday cards. The sight of the cardinal flitting over a horse-drawn sleigh and snow-covered hills set my mental gears spinning. "Gram, I have an urge to be around horses again." I wrapped my arms around my body. "It's so strong, I can't stand it!" I smiled, and my grandmother gazed at me with knowing eyes.

"Don't plan too big, Peaches," she warned. "Remember, I'm in a wheelchair."

I dismissed her concern with a wave of my hand. "I've got something in mind we can all do." I reached for the phone book. I was remembering West Country Farms. We used to drive there in the summertime to stock up on fresh corn and strawberries. The expansive estate was forty-five minutes away from our urban development. Surely they had a winter activity that would be perfect for a seventy-something senior, a four-year-old boy, and a busy single mom whose muscles had gone a tad flabby.

The more I thought about my idea I knew that it would be an experience we could share together. It would give Gram a taste of those past memories that now came to her only in dreams. For one afternoon she could be around horses again, and smell the smells and hear the sounds of the farm she'd relinquished. The escapade would give Justin his first equine adventure, too. Both of my favorite people agreed to participate in this holiday surprise.

It turned out to be everything I dreamed it would be. On that cold December day, Gram and Justin got the chance to "love on" some horses. I held my son up so he could throw his small arms around the neck of one of the draft horses that pulled the jingle-belled sleigh. Gram lovingly and tenderly patted the animal's side.

"Horsies," murmured Justin.

"Big horsies," echoed his Grandma. "Justin, I'll tell you all about this kind of horse later."

Our driver helped Gram ease herself out of her wheelchair and into the sleigh. The three of us, dressed warmly in overcoats, hats, scarves, mittens, and boots, snuggled under a thick down comforter. Only our eyes and noses were exposed, and we knew we'd warm those noses up soon enough at the end of the half-hour ride. Coffee and hot cocoa awaited us back at the farmhouse kitchen, along with heaping servings of warm pie.

The inch of fresh snow that had fallen the night before added to the beauty of the landscape. We felt confident in our driver's ability, and he shouted over his shoulder the names of the farmsteads we passed as the sleigh glided over the country lanes. Wreaths and strings of lights decorated the well-maintained houses, and we imagined them lit at nightfall.

"This is country living!" Gram cried with glee, and my heart leapt with joy to see her happiness at that moment. I hugged my two loved ones close. As I breathed in the crisp air, I felt a great sense of contentment. This old-fashioned sleigh ride was just what I needed to recharge my spirits.

Back in the city, my grandmother clasped my hands and planted a trembling kiss on my cheek. "Thank you, Cherie," she said, stroking my hands. "Thank you for today." She paused. "It was great goin' back to where the horses are."

"Happy holidays, Gram," I said, hugging her in return. "And thanks for being such a good companion to Justin. He's so excited about seeing those horses, he'll probably talk your ear off for days."

She smiled. "What are grandmas for?"

—Cheryl E. Williams

Terrible Trina

During the summer between my freshman and sophomore years at university four decades ago, I found work at an equestrian center. I had always wanted a horse, but my family lived in a city. We had no pasture, couldn't afford the expense of boarding, and didn't have time to drive out to the country more than once or twice a week. So I had learned to ride by taking a lesson every Saturday morning on a rented horse. Despite the commute, my temporary job was the perfect way to earn college money and indulge my love of horses at the same time.

Wednesdays through Sundays, I drove to a facility with two barns and a large, covered riding ring bordered by pastures and a state park. I mucked four box stalls every morning. The three in the upper barn housed privately owned geldings. These boys were handsome, spirited Thoroughbreds, relatively dependable on trails or in dressage or jumping classes, not flighty or neurotic from training at the track.

My fourth horse, Trina, was a dumpy bay mare of around twenty and no clear pedigree. She resided in the old barn as a member of the rental string. Her disposition, I soon learned, was a maddening mix of high intelligence and low humor. And because she often faked lameness to avoid walking, trotting, and cantering in circles for hours with children bouncing on her back, battering her sides with their heels and jerking her mouth with their hands, she had far too much leisure time available.

"You got assigned to take care of Trina?" the experienced barn girls said, laughing. "Oh, Shelly, poor thing. You're in for it." When I asked why, they answered only, "You'll see."

My first hour or two with Trina didn't seem so terrible. She stood in her stall, tail swishing lazily, watching the world from behind a metal mesh gate that I should have realized was put there for good reason. "She bites," a little kid had told me.

Trina blinked her big, brown eyes innocently. I went to the office to see if she had been reserved for classes. I thought it odd that she hadn't been. Everyone else in the rental string had at least two appointments daily. I checked the pasture schedule to see if there were any openings. Full-board horses got first dibs on playing outside. To prevent problems that might end up requiring a vet's visit, every horse went into one of four pastures alone for an hour. The worst trouble they could get into, theoretically, was biting each other over the fence.

I spied one pasture slot open that afternoon, and filled in the vacancy with Trina's name. Maybe, I thought, a change of scene and routine would mellow the old lady. When the time came, I unclipped the metal gate, slid under her stall guard, buckled on her halter, and snapped on the shank. The moment Trina's hooves hit the gravel road, the sleepy plow horse began capering like a stunt kite. Tail high, neck arched, she spun in circles, shaking her head and snorting.

"Are you turning her out?" one of the other barn girls asked. "Trust me. You don't want to do that."

"I don't?"

"She rolls—every single time."

Trina's coat was not the cleanest, shiniest brown. In fact, in this establishment where dirt or sweat marks were heavily frowned on, Trina's flanks were anything but well brushed. Her mane and tail were ratty, neither nicely pulled nor entirely free of straw. And her white socks needed a good bleaching to rid them of their green manure stains.

"You'll never catch her," another girl told me, "not even with treats." Both shook their heads, "She's too smart."

I was beginning to understand. Immediately, Trina helped school me further by nibbling my back pocket, which I thought was sweet until she grabbed the fabric—and a little underlying flesh—with her teeth, jerked her head, and flipped me entirely around, dropping me at her feet. Too late, I remembered that little kid's words from my first day.

Hip stinging but determined, I scrambled up, took a good grip on Trina's shank, and led her off. She squealed the instant I opened the gate, and nearly dragged me into a puddle. In self-defense, I let her loose. Off she ran, bucking like the rankest rodeo bronco, to a patch of bare dirt and mud where she rolled until she was utterly filthy. This did not bode well for me, as we were expected to stay until our horses were clean and fed, their tack spotless, and their stalls free of droppings before we left for the evening.

The other girls were right. Hours passed, and Trina raced away whenever I came close to haltering her. At four o'clock, I fed and watered the horses in the smaller barn, measuring out grain as they nickered contentedly. After a posse of six barn hands failed to help me nab Trina, I decided she would spend the night in the pasture.

I needn't have worried so much about catching her. When I arrived the next morning, a section of fence was knocked down and splintered to bits. Trina was busily working away at the bungee cords meant to keep mice out of the oat bin. So intent was she that I caught her easily, led her to her stall, and locked her in.

After several of us reset the posts and nailed up new rails, I mucked the other stalls, turned the gray gelding out, exercised both chestnuts, sponged and put up their tack, then set off to deal with Trina. She was not a horse who made cleaning a stall easy. Even tied, she kept getting in the way, aiming her hindquarters at me, ears swiveling like radar antennas, heavy hooves prancing as close to the pitchfork tines as a Scottish sword dancer. Grooming her was worse. When I began to pick her feet, she shifted away, tried to bite my bottom, and then leaned all over me. She tried to stomp my toes and swished her tail in my face. I put her in cross-ties in the aisle and wondered what had made her so difficult.

She wasn't mean, I thought, but bored or perhaps lonely. She had plenty of mileage on her. Perhaps because she had once been someone's beloved mare and was now aging among the rental string, she had grown shrewd in her relations with humans, most of whom she could easily bully. In spite of myself, I liked her spunk. Compared to the three unimaginative geldings, Trina was all flair. I gave her half a carrot from my lunch.

And so we began to test each other, trying to settle the "who's-the-boss" contest. Within a week Trina realized she would miss out on her evening oats if I turned her out at four o'clock, and she wasn't in by five. In no time I could catch her, even when I took her to pasture earlier. She began to follow me up the road like a foal after its dam. Sometimes she even rubbed her cheek or forehead against my back or shoulder. Strictly speaking, this behavior should have been corrected, but any sign of affection from Trina seemed like a step in the right direction.

Other than that hour outside once or twice a week, however, she was getting no exercise. No one wanted to ride her. Either she faked being lame, bucked, or bit your butt if you couldn't mount her with lightning speed. Even if you managed to get a leg over her and spur her to class, she either stopped at the entrance to the ring, ears pinned, refusing to budge, or she took the bit in her teeth, bolted away full tilt, and propped until her burden became airborne.

She was a funny old girl. Everyone was surprised when Trina began to behave better for me. Maybe she recognized an equally stubborn spirit. At any rate, when I arrived each morning, I found her standing in a huge hole she dug every night below her stall guard. It was annoying, but I preferred digging to cribbing, the lone bad habit Trina didn't have. Even with a hole so deep she could have escaped into the state park, she never went anywhere, but waited, ears pricked, nickering for me and the apple or carrot I always brought. I'd shovel the dirt and rocks back into the hole, thinking cement might be the ticket, but never suggesting it. After all, Trina had found a relatively harmless way to pass her sleepless nights.

One day, I decided to tack her up and take her on the trails during my lunch hour. Like all the other riders, I was afraid she'd run away with me, buck me off, or leave me wrapped unconscious around a tree. For once, I put on a helmet, which we were always supposed to wear in the park but rarely did. Then Trina and I had the usual combat—she wouldn't let me slip in the bit, which meant I had to take the bridle apart, hang from her ears, grab her tongue, and wrench her jaws apart. She bloated when I tightened the girth. At last, we were both dressed and ready. I flew on before she could even consider biting. When we headed not for the ring but up the sunny path into the woods, both of Trina's ears went forward. She climbed eagerly with the lovely, long overstepping stride of a much younger horse.

All her annoying behaviors gradually disappeared as the summer months passed. I was both delighted but heartbroken early in the autumn when she was sold to a dude ranch. I had to console myself with the thought that she would spend all her time in pasture or on trail rides, which she loved.

On our last day together, I brushed her after an hour spent in the woods. She was lean now, and muscular. Her coat glistened a deep and lustrous mahogany, her black mane and tail were nicely pulled and shiny, her socks bright white. She loaded with no fuss, her soft nostrils breathing moist warmth onto my palm where it offered a final treat. Then the truck pulled away. Trina whinnied once, and I never saw her again.

Another horse moved into her stall, but like the three far more expensive registered Thoroughbreds, I remember next to nothing about him. He didn't dig holes. He wasn't hard to catch or bridle or saddle. He didn't bite or dance toward my toes with his big hooves, go "lame" when he didn't want to work, or step energetically onto the trail in the park, his entire body telling me of his delight in the gift of an hour's pleasure.

It was four decades ago, and yet I recall Terrible Trina best. I still live in a city, and have never had my own horse. At one time, I would have passed her over in an instant, opting for any one of the three Thoroughbreds. Now, though, I recall swinging onto Trina's broad, sometimes bare, back after we learned to trust each other, gripping her warm body with my knees, moving through the dappled sunlight of deep forest, happy in each other's company. Once shown respect, she was generous and sweet. She taught me that appearance isn't everything; that love sometimes comes only after patient effort, and that succeeding at something difficult, in the long run, lasts a lifetime.

—IRENE WANNER

Horseplay

My teenaged fantasies involved a variation on the knight-in-shining-armor story. My knight was a handsome Scottish lad of few words. Strong and capable, he'd gallop into my thoughts on his large, white steed—a fitting mount for a fellow of his stature, which, of course, was high. Perched atop a sleek mare, I'd meet him in a heather-covered glen. There was no need for words. I was content simply to watch his expert fingers smooth his horse's mane in long loving strokes and dream that one day those fingers would stroke my hair.

Invariably, my mother would interrupt my fantasy. In a high-pitched voice that would make every chicken, goat, cow, and hog take cover from our farm to Rocheport several miles away, she'd cry, "Betsy Lou-oh-do-leddy-hoo! Time for dinner!" Nothing ended my fantasizing quicker than that call, perfected by the would-be hog-calling champ of Boone County, Missouri, who also fancied herself a decent yodeler.

I begged my mom to let me go on a month's vacation with my best friend Janet during our summer break. Janet's grandmother boarded horses on her dairy farm in Springfield. My mom balked at first. There was too much work to be done during that time of year—putting up hay, harvesting the gardens, canning. And there was that potato bug infestation—she counted on me to help her pick the bugs off the plants every morning. (God, was there anything I hated worse than that?) But after Janet's mother had a little chat with her, my mom caved in and let me go. Maybe she thought it would be good for me to get away from all those books I'd been reading about Celtic lore and horses. Or maybe she was tired of my cocky attitude. She helped me pack and promised that when I came back at the end of August, we'd go to the state fair in Sedalia. "I'm pretty sure they have a yodeling contest," she told me. "Wouldn't it be great if I won?" I asked Janet if there was any way we could leave right then.

Janet's grandmother's farm was much larger than ours, and I was impressed that she actually owned it. The place included fields, forests, and lots of rugged, wide-open space dotted with cows and horses. I felt as if I belonged, and I could sense good things were coming. Perhaps I'd dreamed about being on that farm, because every twist and turn in the terrain seemed familiar, and so did Mac, the yellow gelding I rode each evening at sunset. Mac wasn't the youngest horse in the barn, and he had a bit of a swayback. Okay, a slight limp, too. I excused his imperfections; we all have them. I tried to imagine my Scottish lad looking at me riding Mac instead of the mare. It could work, I thought, if I could let go of perfection and tweak my fantasy. Astride Mac, I was transformed from a coarse, callused farm girl into a pretty young lass, who no knight in his right mind could resist.

Then I met Freddie Tanner. His father owned the land next to Granny's farm. One day, Freddie asked to join us on our ride. I looked at his freckled face, big ears, and buzz-cut hair, but before I could make up an excuse, Janet opened her big mouth and said yes, but only if Freddie would bring along his older brother Brian. I should have seen what was coming.

At sunset, the four of us galloped to a big rock where Janet and I always met whenever we went exploring. She rode off with Brian, and I was stuck with Freddie. Thank goodness for Mac. I never fawned over a horse so much in my life. While Mac kept his feelings for me hidden, Freddy acted as if he was the world's greatest gift to a thirteen-year-old girl. My disgust grew as I watched him pick at a scab on his elbow. He knew it repulsed me, but he just grinned and kept right on picking it until it bled.

I took Mac to a nearby pond for a drink. Freddie followed with his horse. When he was close enough to touch me, he puckered up his chubby lips and leaned over. I darted under Mac's neck. Mac snorted and pawed while I sought safe haven on higher ground a short distance away. "Good ol' boy, Mac," I whispered. "Drink your fill, and we're out of here." I challenged Freddie to a race I never intended to win. While he bounced on his horse toward some imaginary finish line, I nudged Mac and headed straight back to the barn.

When Janet got home, she yelled at me for leaving Freddy out there by himself. I wanted to know what that big ugly stain on her neck was. We didn't speak for the next few days. Even worse, Freddy's disgusting face kept interrupting my fantasy.

Granny was a church-going woman. One Saturday night, she insisted we accompany her to the local Baptist church for its annual pie supper and fundraiser. A cousin would pick us all up in his truck. Janet and I begged her to let us ride the horses instead, and to our surprise, she agreed. But she looked straight at Janet's neck and warned us against any funny stuff.

If Granny had known that Janet was going to pull off her dressy cowgirl shirt and show off her newly grown cleavage in a low-cut halter-top, she would never have let us go. It was a hundred degrees, but Janet piled on the layers like it was winter. It was pretty obvious to me that she and Brian planned to ditch the pie supper and ride off someplace where he could suck on her neck and lord-only-knows-what-else. She didn't give a second thought to leaving me with Freddie. This vacation was not turning out like I'd hoped.

But things started to look up when I arrived at the churchyard and got a glimpse of Tom O'Malley. Tom was Janet's cousin and had brought their grandmother to the church. Suddenly, I wondered how I could convince Janet's grandmother to ride Mac home.

A pie supper is an old rural tradition wherein each woman packs a homemade pie into a box, and the men bid on the boxes—and the bakers. The winning bidder then goes off with the woman to share the goodies in the box. I hoped Tom would pick mine, but he chose the box brought by the preacher's daughter. Freddie must have seen me carrying my box to the table because, wouldn't you know, he bid on it until he got the box—and me—for the evening. While all the other boxes were being distributed, I stayed close to Mac and whispered my unhappiness about spending the evening with Freddy. I stroked Mac like my fantasy knight stroked his white steed. And when Freddy asked me where we could go, private-like, to eat, I hemmed and hawed. Then Mac, God love him, shifted his weight and set his hoof right down on

Freddie's foot. Freddie let out a yodel better than any sound my mother ever made.

Freddie's father took him to the doctor, so I was free to turn my attention to Tom. *Man, would he ever look good on a white steed!* As I gathered apples and leftover carrots for Mac, who deserved a big treat, Tom turned and smiled at me. My heart raced the entire journey home. I was eager to wash and change my clothes before the fair-skinned Scottish-looking Tom brought Granny home. Back at the farm, I brushed Mac for an hour and promised him a bath the next day. When Janet showed up she said that Brian's parents had caught her and Brian necking and told Brian he couldn't see her anymore. She was too young. I thought they were right, and the two of us started arguing. Somehow in the midst of the argument, her grandmother arrived, and Tom O'Malley left. My anger turned to tears. I consoled myself with the thought that I'd surely see him again. But as fate would have it, I never did. For a summer or two thereafter, whenever I picked bugs off the potato leaves or helped my mom can green beans, Tom O'Malley would slip into my mind. He'd gallop toward me on a white steed where I waited astride Mac in a heather-covered glen. I don't know if he ever married the preacher's daughter, but if he'd asked me to marry him that summer when I was thirteen, I would have said yes.

—Meera Lester

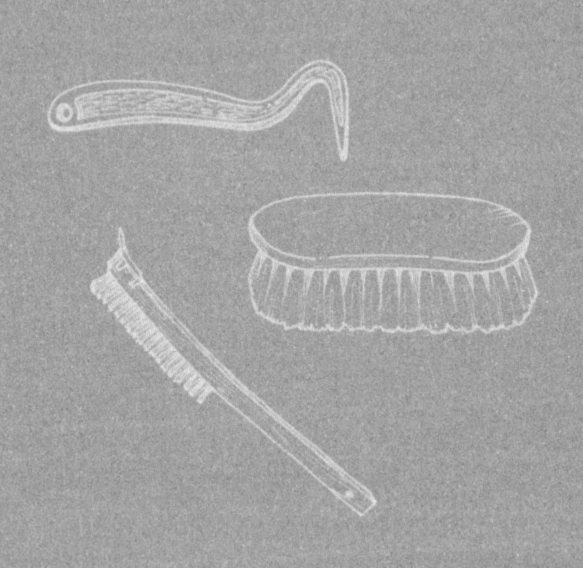

My Old Man

I got to the ranch around eight that Saturday morning toward the end of summer. Though it was early, it was already hot, with the promise of more heat to come. I parked under a eucalyptus tree the bright yellow survey truck I'd bought from my father. The heat intensified the tree smell—a soothing, dusty cold-lozenge, and I breathed it in. From the truck bed I hoisted out my groom box, a halter, and a bag of carrots. I set them on a log bench under a pepper tree in the barnyard. I waved hello to Marcie, the ranch owner, as she navigated her golf cart toward the milking shed, a nanny goat trotting along behind.

In the corral, my old man turned away from his breakfast and nickered low and throatily. He made his way to the gate with a sort of half crab, half motorboat motion and nodded his head at me. I nodded back. When I opened his gate, he moved past me without waiting for the old leather halter. I draped it over my arm.

This halter is one of the pieces of tack that came with my old man. Five years ago, his former owner decided that she no longer wanted to pay for his upkeep and instructed his caregiver to "find him a home or have him put down." I volunteered to give him a home.

This handsome chestnut gelding had been a jumper in his youth and retrained in dressage in his mature years. It wasn't surprising that he'd gone lame, living in a box stall as he had for nearly two decades. Slowly I nursed him back to soundness with four months of hand walking and two months of easy work under saddle. I had his neglected teeth fixed and introduced supplements to his diet and an occasional massage for his old muscles.

I sliced half a dozen carrots into his feed dish as he waited patiently under the pepper tree. The carrots smelled appealing. I bit into one and worked the gritty, sweet root around in my mouth. From the barrel near his shelter, I added a coffee-can measure of senior feed, dense-smelling stuff full of corn and molasses, to fatten his old bony self before winter came and he got too cold.

There were plenty of other horses on the ranch, including my retired mare and young gelding, but my old man had ended up by himself because he needed special care: a daily gram of bute dissolved in applesauce (to make it palatable) added to his feed. I stirred this recipe in with the carrots. His mare friends and the weanling colt in the south pasture couldn't be expected to let him take his medicine, disguised as it was, without butting in for a bite of their own. Even the goats ran him off his food, I mused as I set his dish down on a sliced round of eucalyptus trunk. My old man began to eat as I opened the groom box and took out a complement of good brushes.

Three or four years ago, after I'd nursed him back to health, I decided to take my old man out of his box-stall situation. I brought him to this ranch where I had come to camp as a kid. Back then my father had thought the rustic atmosphere, with stalls to muck and horses to ride, would do me good—and it did. I figured it would do my old horse some good, too, and when he first arrived he'd been the happiest I'd ever seen him. He babysat the weanling foals; they took to him like a venerable old uncle, and he took to them in kind. But after a couple seasons of too much roughhousing, and a fall from which he never quite recovered, my old man began to do poorly. Sometimes when I visited him, he couldn't lift his chin higher than his knees.

From time to time when he walked, he couldn't control his momentum to slow down. He reminded me of my eighty-year-old father, who has Parkinson's. He might get going down the street in one direction, hunched and determined, but then not be able to slow down or control his turns. He'd end up ashamed, pulling up short before stepping into traffic.

One day in particular, my old horse's discomfort and humiliation brought me to tears. When I went to catch this usually easy-to-catch fellow in the pasture, I whistled his special whistle. I called to him by one of his many endearing nicknames, "Goo'b'y" or "Uncle G." He swung around, bobbed his head, and slowly came along. When he started out he was quite a distance away, but he gradually picked up speed as he ambled in my direction. Then, as if he'd made a change of plan, he veered to the left and ended up just shy of where I stood at the gate. He blinked and regarded me out of the corner of his eye. I approached him, put the halter on, and asked him to step back in order to negotiate the turn toward the exit. But when I touched his chest and applied a little pressure, he shuddered and nearly crumbled backwards. His hind end wasn't responding at all to where he wanted his front feet to go.

I didn't cry in front of him. I wanted to spare him that indignity, just as when something like that happens with my father, and I give him a pat and make a halfhearted comment, "Come on, Pops, let's go get something to eat." I did cry on the ride home, though, and called the vet, who promised to come out the following week. If I had to have my horse put down, I needed to prepare myself.

As I waited for the vet to arrive a few days later, I envisioned various scenarios involving "humane euthanasia," a term I loathe, yet couldn't seem to get out of my mind. But after the vet finished his evaluation, he assured me that my old man just needed more meat on his bones and a gram of bute daily. And because he needed to eat his fill and take his medicine undisturbed, I had decided to separate my old man from his friends. I regretted it—it was one of the small parts of his life that he loved—but what could I do?

Poor fellow, I thought as I picked out his favorite brushes: the plastic-tipped human hairbrush and the array of stiff- or soft-bristled horse brushes that fit various tasks. I began to work on his coat as he chewed his snack. The hairbrush loosened the dried sweat-and-dirt compound that striped his hind end from croup to stifle. The stuff loosened in puffs, which brought with them tufts of coat from places where he hadn't yet shed. It seemed he spent the whole season shedding.

I applied some elbow grease with the hairbrush and got the bristles down to my old man's hide. When I curried certain spots, he'd chew or push his snack around his dish, choosing bites grain by grain; in other spots, he'd hesitate, and as I insisted with my brush, he'd slowly lift his head, close his eyes, and stretch his neck long in an expression I call "foal face," curling his lip away from his gum. He'd shudder blissfully as I worked slowly around the area until his itch gave up some of its intensity.

As I brushed, I could feel the effects of the additional hay and senior feed on his ribs. He was plumping a bit. And, thanks to the bute, he was moving as freely as I'd seen him in two months. He was feeling better. Giving up his friends had been a good tradeoff, at least in this respect, but still I wondered how he'd fare in winter. His corral didn't have a run-in shed, just a bit of a lean-to next to the feed bin. I knew that blanketing him nightly would be a hardship for Marcie, especially if it rained and the blanket got soaked and muddy.

My old man finished his snack. I asked him if I could go over his face with a soft cloth, and he let me remove bits of crusty stuff from his eyes and nostrils and bits of grain from his whiskered chin. Then I gave him a final all-over dusting and his chestnut coat shone copper.

"You're a good old man," I said to him, and he followed me back to his pen. I patted his rump as he wandered over to the far corner where he could just see his friends beyond the eucalyptus grove. I balanced on the fence a while, breathing in horse and pepper tree and eucalyptus. The morning's heat had intensified, and it warmed my back as I watched my old man watch his friends. A little breeze blew a scatter of leaves in a knot. I began to consider moving my old man closer to home, where I could see him every day and where he could spend time in closer proximity to other horses.

I didn't know offhand of any good boarding place closer to home, but I would start to ask around. This day at the end of summer was a good one for us. I thought of my father. It might do him good to spend a little time with this old man. I swung off the fence and packed up my stuff, combing the brushes out one by one as I put them back into the box. My old man left his corner, strolled to the water trough, and drank in long satisfying gulps. Then he came over to watch me pack, nickering hopefully for a last carrot.

—Charlotte Davidson

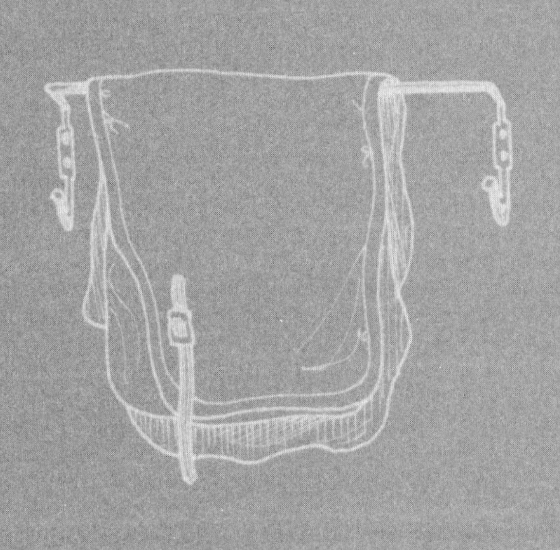

Looking for Mr. Right

When I was a girl, I pined for a horse. I spent hours drawing them, loudly whining for them, and staring off into space imagining how *perfect* my life would be when I had one. In my imagination, my horse had a silken mane and muscles that rippled beneath a coat of polished obsidian. I'd read *The Black Stallion*. I'd seen Triple-Crown-winner Citation with my own eyes. I knew that horses were glossy and streamlined, that they intuited your every command, and that they stayed loyal and steadfast for life.

When I got older, I pined for a boyfriend. I spent hours doodling my future last name in notebooks, silently pleading with Tom or Steve to notice me, and staring off into space imagining how *perfect* my life would be when I had one. In my imagination, my boyfriend read literature and never gawked at the cheerleaders. Well into my adulthood, I still expected the man of my dreams to lavish me with baubles, feed me peeled grapes, and adore me to my dying day. In my more delusional moments, it all happened on horseback.

Decades older and still horseless, with several failed relationships notched in my belt, I'd pretty much given up finding Mr. Right. So one fall day, I decided to indulge in the more attainable fantasy.

I found a nonprofit that combined horses, the outdoors, and an activity that seemed truly worthwhile. The facility provided physical therapy on horseback to disabled youngsters and adults. I volunteered to help.

Unlike most horse-crazy girls, I'd never owned a horse or even spent much time around them. To me, they were conjectural, like a man who surprises you with rose petals and diamonds. And, as in the man fantasy, they were perfect in every detail.

My first day at the therapy center was in chilly October. I arrived early and eagerly looked into the stalls. Far from my reverie's delicate, high-strung Arabians, these dozen or so chunky beasts wore shaggy winter coats. If they noticed me at all, it was with mild interest, not an instant and deeply felt bond. With patients due to arrive any minute, the staff had its hands full just making sure that the horses were fed and watered, the wood shavings were brushed off them, and they were tacked up for the sessions. That first day the horses did their job—walking slowly and carefully, and I did mine—making sure the kids didn't fall off. I left feeling exhilarated just being around these creatures, and as comfortable as if I'd been around them my whole life.

My second week, I brought apples to win over my new equine friends. I patted Ben's pale cheek as he and I listened to the other horses nose their hay. The stolid American Cream reminded me of my first serious boyfriend, whom I met at my first serious job in my twenties. As tall as a plow horse, farm raised, and dependable, he talked slightly less than Ben did. He never lost his temper, uttered a word of endearment, or alluded to a long-term commitment. Nothing ever changed. Sensible, hardworking, and placid, he plodded on.

I held out a piece of apple for Ben. He lifted his head to the side and eyed it before taking it gently. Horses rely on their sense of smell to detect a morsel held under their muzzles. Even their fantastically panoramic range of vision won't let them see that point right above their upper lip. That first boyfriend wasn't able to see what was smack in front of his nose, either. My stellar qualities went unacknowledged, and my attention drifted. Wanting more, I looked for greener pastures.

I saw other women with flashy rides and expensive trappings. Maybe that's why I was so susceptible in my thirties when an old high-school friend unexpectedly reappeared. He lived in another state, but we spent hours commiserating on the phone. Frequent letters suggested the intimacy I'd been missing. After a seaside rendezvous that promised a storybook future of romance and escape, I galloped halfway across the country with him faster than you could say *giddyup!*

As the weeks passed at the therapy center, I got to know the horses as individuals. Odie, a stocky Haflinger the color of a gingerbread cookie, was described as a perpetual adolescent, and I soon learned why. Odie craves attention and food. When denied either, he bangs on his metal stall door with his metal-clad hoof. I jumped the first time I heard the sharp, deafening ring, which I'm sure was his intent. Come too close, and his lips search for morsels, sleeves, fingers—anything that might be construed as edible. In a therapy session, however, with a small child on his back, Odie is the epitome of gentlemanly perfection. With horses, as with men, looks can be deceiving.

The relationship with Mr. Pseudo Romantic lasted three years—exactly two years and eight months too long. Lured by the promise of togetherness, the reality couldn't have been more different. My early morning schedule didn't synch with his late nights. When he wasn't working, he slept more than Seabiscuit. Nightclubs and massage parlors proved more alluring to him than anything he could find at home. Eventually Mr. Pseudo's insidious form of psychological abuse made me feel like a wild mustang caught in a snare. On the verge of gnawing off my leg to escape, I was rescued when a dear friend offered me a place to board temporarily.

Horses grab with their rubbery, prehensile lips. I've never been bitten by any of the horses, even when I forget to flatten my palm. Carnivores grab with their teeth. Mr. Pseudo, I see now, was a carnivore. My ego and psyche suffered many wounds when he lashed out with words or actions. I watched Odie and wondered, where are the men who accept you the way a horse accepts a treat—gratefully, carefully, and with undisguised enthusiasm?

Just forty and still champing at the bit to find love, I tried the personal ads. It wasn't much different from buying a horse: You look at a lot of homely, lame, and skittish plugs before you find the one animal you can commit to. And just as an experienced horseman can size up a mount from across the paddock, each date's eyes would sweep over my conformation, his mind already made up before I opened my mouth. Unfortunately, after thirty first dates I learned to do the same. I quickly found out that "sandy hair" didn't necessarily mean "on the head." To my credit, I never examined anyone's teeth to determine his real age. When I finally met a man I was attracted to, who had brains, spirit, and the allure of a rock star, I suspected he might be too much for me. Equestrians call this "overmounted." Temporarily blinded, I leaped over my better judgment in hot pursuit.

One day at the stable, Harley lifted his head high and studied me with what looked like haughty amazement. The buckskin Paso Fino mix has attitude. Harley is blonde and attractive and thinks he owns the world, as most blonde and attractive people do. He likes to pull down zippers. When Odette, one of the horse handlers, tapped his leg with her crop, he picked it up. She did the same with a hind leg, and he lifted that. He'll keep this up until he looks as if he's dancing.

Mr. Wannabe Rock Star resembled a glitzy show horse creeping past his prime, yet still performing the same old tricks. He refused to discard his studied "bad boy" image, despite thinning hair and advancing age. No equine star of the Spanish Riding School ever primped for a performance the way this fellow dyed, sprayed, and shellacked the shoulder-length mane receding from his forehead. He had the muscular build of a stallion and the aloof demeanor to match. Ultimately, not even expensive dinners or a trip to the Virgin Islands could compensate for his clandestine nuzzling of not one, but a herd of girlfriends.

One day another horse handler, Benedicte, called me into the barn. "Are you a horse brusher, Anita?" I admitted that I'd never brushed a horse in my life. She asked if I'd ever led a horse. I was almost ashamed to admit that I hadn't. She handed me the lead rope and showed me where to hold it near Six's chin and how to fold—not coil—the rope in my left hand.

"Do you know how to tie him up?" No again. "Do you knit?" I did. The loose knot that you use to tie a horse to a fence bears a resemblance to a stitch cast on a needle. If the horse pulls on its end, the rope stays tight. But if you pull on the other end, it comes undone in a flash. All men know about this quick-release mechanism. Just when I think that love or shared interests bind us together, they know how to jerk the loose end of the rope and bolt. Tied up, tied down, they'll have none of it, while there I stand, helpless to free myself from my broken dreams.

Benedicte handed me the brush, and I dusted Six from head to hooves. She showed me how to cluck and touch his flank to make him move over, and I brushed his other side.

"Six doesn't like to be girthed," she said as she tightened the band under his belly. He vigorously bobbed his head in agreement.

"Why?" I asked, still the novice.

"Imagine being slowly strangled," Benedicte's eyes twinkled. Six nodded. His resemblance to my commitment-phobic boyfriends was uncanny.

Once Six got to know me better, he took to rubbing his nose on the front of my sweatshirt. I was told that was his way of showing he liked me. I've experienced more ambiguous signs of affection from men. One gave me a book about garbage for Christmas. It's too bad I wasn't as good at reading signals back then as I am now.

After Mr. Wannabe, my next relationship came as a relief. He was like an energetic quarter horse, the kind whose ears prick forward when you approach, who willingly crashes through the underbrush to explore a new trail, and who gives his all no matter how high the jump. Mr. Outdoors was garrulous and interested in everything from the blues to books to photography. Our first date comprised a four-hour hike, several games of billiards, and endless talk over a Cuban meal of sea bass and rice. I felt as though I'd won first prize in three-day eventing. He introduced me to sea kayaking and to "wandering." We would drive to a city or wilderness, park the car, and walk for hours. We stayed together for five years, until some of the qualities I found so endearing at first began to wear thin, like the horse whose nips seem playful until those nips grow tiresome and painful.

After several weeks at the therapy center, it dawned on me that I had been looking to the wrong species for my answers. I've tried live-in arrangements, rekindling old friendships, and blink-and-you-miss-him dating, but I have never anticipated a date with a man as much as I look forward to seeing those horses every week. I know they like me. The apples could have something to do with it, but even laden with food or gifts, I never got such a warm and attentive response from a man. Horses and men do have their similarities. Both can be uncommunicative and stubborn. Both are liable to kick when you least expect it. Both eat a lot and demand more attention than a month-old baby. So maybe that means they also share some of the *best* equine qualities.

As I brush Six or laugh at Harley's rakishness, I ponder how different the reality of horses is from my dream. I see now that I wasn't ready for a real horse when I was a child. My daydreams back then didn't include the tender eyes and inquisitive ears that flip back and forth as you talk. They didn't include the warm comfort of a big, fuzzy shoulder. Nor did they include the wonder of a half-ton beast willingly and daintily picking up each hoof so I could scrape out the dirt, as casually as one person shakes hands with another. No, the daydreams paled in comparison to the real thing.

My hope now is that the same holds true for men. Thanks to Ben, Odie, Harley, and Six, I know what I'm looking for. The horses represent my gold standard. The way Harley undresses people by pulling on zippers is a lot more honest than the guy who undresses you with his eyes while he pretends to listen to what you say. Odie knows when to put his adolescent shenanigans aside and get serious. And if I can just find a man who is as friendly and sweet as Six, who listens patiently when I talk, and who looks at me as if I might just be smarter than he is, I'll be set. All my relationships—human and equine—have only prepared me for that one perfect one that I know is in my future. He might not lavish me with baubles or feed me peeled grapes, but he will love me *just because.* And in my more delusional moments, it all happens on horseback.

—A. BRONWYN LLEWELLYN

Just Bless

"I think she needs a *lot* of help!" Stacie described how Bless, the beautiful three-year-old filly, would pin her ears, charge, and bite during feed time. Bless was a "nightmare" to the vet and farrier, and "evil" to her two gelding pasture mates and placid old companion goat. She seemed to bite and kick the other animals just for fun.

Carefully, I peered over the stall door to observe the flashy black-and-white Bless. Alert and curious, she didn't look like such a terror. The story was probably exaggerated, I thought. A firm hand was all that was needed. I suggested we take her into the paddock on a long line.

As we walked the short distance outside, I felt the tension build in the filly. Just as we entered the paddock, she jerked away from me and ran, but I was ready when she hit the end of the line. Bless whirled and charged, rearing a few feet in front of me. I stepped back, and she swapped ends and kicked out furiously. When Stacie hurried in to help, the filly calmed down quickly, so we led her back to the stall without more trouble.

Bless appeared to be a hard-core juvenile delinquent. It was obvious that the only person Bless trusted was Stacie, but that relationship didn't include respect. There was something very intriguing about Bless—an air of great intelligence. I liked her. I sensed her aggression arose from fear rather than meanness. As far as she knew, she was simply protecting herself.

Stacie told me how she had fallen in love with the yearling filly and brought her home dreaming of the beautiful English-type riding horse she would become. She was a spoiled child, but the trainer who took her on as a two-year-old said he'd fix her manners.

The trainer made Stacie promise not to visit Bless at his barn at any time during the training. He told her that her presence would be too distracting for the horse. Three months later, without notice, the trainer unloaded Bless at Stacie's and disappeared in a cloud of dust. He moved to Florida never to be heard from again.

Only then did Stacie discover that her playful, pushy, audacious "baby" had become an aggressive, angry, canny, and very strong horse. Bless treated people and other animals with contempt. There was no way to force her into submission. Anything she did had to be her choice. I needed to show her a better way of living before she ended up in a rodeo or as an entree on a menu far away, or before she killed someone. I didn't usually deal with dangerous horses, but Bless was a different sort of puzzle.

I explained to Stacie that my methods differed from conventional horse training in some special ways. My own experience of many years, and the influence of Linda Tellington-Jones's work, told me that it would be necessary to start Bless's training over.

We also had to help her voluntarily and completely change the way she dealt with frustration and anxiety.

The first hurdle was to get her to my facility. A local expert in difficult loaders had no success and only narrowly escaped injury. I was reluctant to try; as a working mother, I couldn't afford to be hurt. Yet I was beginning to understand how Bless thought. Her crazy behavior was calculated and intelligent. She was not hysterically *out* of control; rather, she counted on being *in* control at all times.

An experienced friend helped me back a large stock trailer into a twelve-foot gate opening. There, we boxed Bless in and slowly pushed her forward into the trailer. Once she sized up the situation, she sensibly stopped fighting and stepped into the trailer calmly. She unloaded just as easily at her new boarding school.

Bless was adept at taking advantage of any perceived weaknesses in others. The first feed time at her new home was the only time she tried to charge anyone. The barn worker coolly stood her ground, pointing out that it's not nice to bite the one who feeds you. Bless got the message.

Leading Bless continued to be a test of patience. There was no getting her to move until she was good and ready. Instead of whacking her or trying to trick her, I started with the TTouch, circling the tips of my fingers on her shoulder or anywhere else that seemed safe. Bemused, she then moved.

Humility was a more difficult lesson, taught to her by a very large, rude warmblood gelding. No other owners wanted their horses out with these two delinquents, so they became turnout partners. The gelding stood, unmoved, while Bless kicked him in the chest as hard as she could. *Is that the best you can do, honey,* he seemed to jeer. Bless returned to the barn somewhat shaken and more thoughtful.

I was very cautious while working on Bless's body, especially around her hindquarters. I made sure that I was calm, unhurried, and grounded. She began to enjoy the TTouches, which are named after the different animals they characterize. Very head shy at first, she became easy to halter after many raccoon touches, or circles, on her face, and llama strokes on her ears. Eventually, I could do the lick-of-the-cow's-tongue around her barrel, along with belly lifts. Python leg lifts followed. When she finally allowed me to pick up her feet and handle them without protest, we began leg circles and stretches.

At first, even the sight of a whip made Bless angry. She would snort, pin her ears, and threaten me. As we worked, I let her get used to seeing the wand lying around, and soon I snuck in some gentle strokes with it along her sides and legs. She soon lost her fear of the whip and was ready and able to follow my signals with it once we began groundwork.

From such a difficult beginning, it was a pleasant surprise to see Bless's rapid progress as we prepared for work under saddle. She was so smart that she learned everything the first time. It was a challenge to keep her interested and happy.

Bless never stopped testing me. One hot day, while fully tacked and working on the long line, she dropped to roll in the sand. When I quickly shooed her to her feet, she charged me in irritation and anger. I first had to apologize to her and then explain why her actions weren't right.

After four months, Bless went home, where I continued working with her and her owner. Stacie learned some of her horse's favorite touches, and it was delightful to see the trust and respect steadily increase between them. But we both had to keep one step ahead of Bless. She was not one to be taken for granted; you had to be honest and direct with her. If you wavered or seemed insincere, she knew instantly. Stacie was a novice and in no way ready to ride such a determined mare, so my task was to train them both, without confrontations or accidents. The arena wasn't fenced off from the rest of the field, so if Bless got bored, she would suddenly zoom off, uphill or down, out of the rider's control.

Bucking was yet another option Bless used to alleviate boredom and maintain the status quo. One day Stacie, Bless, and I were practicing serpentines at the walk. Bless was behaving perfectly. Suddenly I felt fuzzy as I was riding. Everything seemed ethereal and somehow not real. Then I noticed a lot of dirt on my breeches and my helmet brim was crooked. When I asked if Bless had bucked me off, Stacie replied that she had made a good attempt to launch me into outer space. I had hit the ground hard on the return trip, and Stacie said I had been knocked out cold. Bless, rather than leave the scene of the crime—or trample me—carefully checked every inch of my body for vital signs. She shoved me with her nose as if to say, *I'm sorry, I didn't mean to kill you, get up now, so we can play some more.* Stacie said I got to my feet and asked her to help me mount Bless, and I sounded normal. Twenty minutes later, while riding, I "woke up." If Bless had wanted to kill me, she would have had plenty of time to do the job.

Since there was no way we could force Bless into good behavior, I suggested we try some reverse psychology on her. We knew how many seconds Bless was willing to behave properly before livening things up. Getting a feel for the moment when Bless quit listening, I told Stacie to change gait, direction, or both, suddenly and without warning. She could ask Bless to hustle down the slope outside the arena, or take a quick spin around the light pole at either end.

The strategy worked. Bless began to listen very attentively to her rider because, apparently, we liked the same games she did! Soon, training and games became one to her. By keeping Bless entertained, Stacie was able to learn the necessary skills to ride this very spirited mare.

Bless will never change her spots; she remains a proud, clever, wild female that carries herself like a queen. She welcomes Stacie and me with whinnies; everyone else must ask permission to approach. When you feel the power and presence of a horse that cooperates because she enjoys doing so, riding becomes both a thrill and a privilege.

This bold, vivacious mare is a vivid reminder to look beyond the language barrier to the qualities that create understanding between beings: trust, honesty, persistence, courage, and creativity. When Bless turns her head and gives me the eye, she's saying, *Never forget, what you give is what you get!* Thank you, Bless. One more trainer has been trained.

–STAR HUGHES

Only the Best

Lyrical Chant was the textbook version of a good-looking pony: superb conformation, deep chestnut with two white socks and a crisp white blaze. He was fit, schooled, and proven. There was no way that I was going to be given a scrubby little Shetland, or someone's washed-up hack, although that would have been fine with me. In fact, once the decision had been made to get a pony, there was very little talk about it at all. I was getting a pony; my parents were going to decide which pony it was going to be, and that was pretty much all there was to it.

Once the horse shopping began in earnest, I had a vague feeling of unease about the whole thing. The little lectures about how much appreciation I should be showing cropped up here and there on the way to and from viewing the various ponies. After a while, I wondered if I really wanted all of this in the first place. But I was getting a pony. What could be the problem?

Chantsy was a grand pony—everybody said so. I loved going to the barn and admiring him. I spent hours brushing his mane and tail, dusting him down with my new red dandy brush with the stiff, bright bristles, and picking out his feet with the smart blue-handled hoof pick. I'd chosen it myself at the tack store, my favorite place in the whole world: the exotic smell of leather and wool; the bright glitter of shiny bits and picks and harnesses hanging on the wall; the stirrups clanking on the racks, the sheepskin girths, and the delicious smell of neat's-foot oil and soap. All the possibilities dazzled me.

I had been taking group lessons for about a year, at Elly Dodd's barn. I was plunked on a different pony every week. They were a cagey lot, those school nags. They would whip a walleyed head around to snap at my leg or maliciously stamp on my foot while I tacked them up. It was all I could do to thrash my scrawny legs hard enough to startle them into a slovenly trot. But it didn't matter because I was on a horse. Mrs. Dodd's staged little school gymkhanas where we showed off our riding prowess, and with our velvet caps brushed and the dirt washed out of our breeches, we felt like pros. For a couple of glorious hours, those same ornery beasts that drove us to tears of frustration every Saturday became almost noble. At the end of the day, I was trundled home, sweaty and exhausted, with a handful of twenty-five-cent ribbons and a plastic trophy or two to show for it.

The arrival of Chantsy heralded bigger things. I was pretty sure that I was too cowardly and uncoordinated to make it into the big leagues, but the ball was already rolling. Evening talks around the kitchen table suddenly centered on the benefits of this instructor over that one, and I was starting to get nervous.

First on the list was Rudee's Academy. Rudee was one of those taut, wiry no-nonsense equestrians with an indiscernible European accent, descended from a long line of equally indiscernible European equestrians. I had met him a couple of years before, when a friend took lessons at his vast stables. That first meeting, I wandered around slack-jawed, gaping at the eye candy of sleek horses and glowing polished leather and brass. Rudee boosted me onto the back of Ben, the biggest horse I'd ever seen, and clipped a lunge line onto his bridle. I bounced around in agony until Ben broke into a rolling canter, and I rolled right along with him. "She's a real rider, zis one," Rudee called over to my mother. It was the proudest moment of my life.

But now Rudee had morphed into a stern taskmaster, a brisk general in breeches who scrutinized me from the center of the ring. He paced, hands clasped behind his back, tapping his riding crop against his boots. He poked me here, adjusted me there, all business and criticism. My legs were too loose. My seated trot wasn't deep enough. I'd have to work on my balance. My hands were too high. I was crushed. I'd just failed a test that I didn't even know I'd been taking.

Rudee might be just what I needed, my parents said over dinner that night.

Next stop was Kris. Kris lived and breathed horses. She smelled like a horse, and I liked that. She also wore riding clothes every minute of the day, except that hers weren't spotless like Rudee's, and there was a tattered barn coat thrown over the works. She didn't have stable hands to do her dirty work for her. It was a chilly afternoon when Chantsy and I met her. Kris put us through our paces, going through all the gaits and mincing over *cavaletti*. She was kind, and I felt better. Then she pointed to the next paddock where her eight-year-old daughter was smartly rounding the ring on a trim little mare, effortlessly sailing over three-foot fences. They'd just gotten that pony for her last week, she remarked, from a breeder down in the States. They were going to school it for the winter and decide if they were going to take it on the show circuit next spring. This was serious business. I was in way over my head. All I wanted to do was ride a horse.

Kris had Rudee beat, hands down, my parents concluded that night.

Family finances were tight, though, so rather than pay for lessons, my father started measuring and marking out the small paddock beside the barn. The lessons were going to be at home, and my father was going to be my instructor.

This turned out to be a very bad idea. I think it was all because my helmet was too small. I tried to tell them this, but I was told to stop being ridiculous and get in the saddle. Whatever the reason, I would develop blinding headaches during my twice-weekly riding lessons. I was frustrated and miserable, and my head hurt. I wanted to be at the pool. I wanted to be playing Barbies or climbing trees with the girl next door. I wanted to be hanging out in the barn, playing with kittens in the dusky hayloft or brushing down Chantsy. I wanted to be his friend. Instead, we were turning into enemies.

It all ended late that summer. "Aren't you interested in riding any more?" my parents asked, not kindly. But I'd already figured out that if they'd already formulated the answer that they wanted me to give them, it was best to just give them that answer. I was stuck. Protesting and trying to explain would lead to bad results all around. I had tried to tell them that my helmet was squeezing my brains out, and that had gotten nowhere. I still loved riding, but their definition of riding and mine differed wildly. I didn't want to be the best. I just wanted to be able to get on my pony and ride at dusk, when the house and barn lights were starting to glow, and the crickets were loud in the long grass near the barn doors. I wanted to go out to his stall on a cold winter morning and feel Chantsy snuffle into my face, and just smell him. I didn't realize that there was a price tag attached to all this that an eleven-year-old couldn't afford to pay.

"No, I don't think I am interested in riding any more."

There were explosions and then an icy calm that was even worse than the storm. I guess it must have been a few weeks later that I was packed off to someone's house for the night, a friend's or a relative's, I can't remember. When I came home, Chantsy was gone. All that was given in the way of explanation were biting comments, reproachful looks, and that empty, mocking stall. And that was the end of my riding career.

About twelve years later, I was home for a visit when I saw Chantsy's old red-bristled dandy brush. My sister had found it in the tack room and was using it on her pony, a beautiful gray. By that time, I had taken up riding again, once a week at a stable outside of the city where I lived. We were all adults in the group, all one rung above slightly hopeless, and we all loved to ride just for the hell of it. Classes were followed by a cold beer in the tack room, where we could sit back, talk horse talk, and breathe in the smells of the barn.

It had taken years for horses and me to find each other again, and this time we were on equal footing. They weren't an obligation or an expectation. They were a choice. I had come back to the place that I had found with Ben all those years before: the simple joy of being on a horse.

—PAULA CORBETT

From Horseback

I float through knee-high grasses, seed tassels wavering as I walk the pasture. Indian blanket blossoms, red centers afire, share the field with black-eyed Susans, gumdrop eyes on buttery petals. The spring grasses whisper as I part them, and I wonder why any horse would leave this place.

Slipping through the two gates, I find halters, colors faded from wind and sun, hanging on the wooden fence post. Three chestnut geldings in the field glance at me for a moment and return to the grass. Manny, a reddish-bay with a black mane and sunburned auburn tail, pauses his grazing for the spongy carrot I offer as small payment for the work he'll do. He takes the treat and gives it a cautious chew while I pull the green halter over his nose.

I turn toward the gate, and Manny follows me without protest, remembering that we are old friends. Small orange moths flit up as we walk. I maneuver the gelding through the gates without looking back, knowing he'll twist his body around like a cat and shimmy through the opening. He'll follow me to the barn, then to one of the arenas for jumping or dressage work.

Kirsten, her ponytail pulled tight through a baseball cap, rides up on a bay mare. Horse and rider move together in a lanky walk, both blowing hard from the movements they've practiced. "I'm about to wash her off and grab Taylor," says Kirsten, patting the mare. "Want to go on a trail ride?"

I stop Manny and shade my eyes to look up at Kirsten. Because Manny is mud-free, I would spend five minutes on grooming and a few more to saddle up. Next, we would go through our dressage paces, making round circles and precise transitions. I look at Manny's quiet eye and then back at Kirsten. Trail riding is also work, I reason, "Sure."

Cars crowd the highway, inches between their bumpers. A semi groans into a lower gear, its twin smoke spires making it a dragon. My window, open for spare breezes, captures hot exhaust.

A green sedan fills the rear-view mirror. The face silhouetted behind me distorts in frustration over a destination too difficult to reach in afternoon traffic. I can't go any faster, so I try to think of fields and horses. He whips his car around mine to sit beside me in the next lane.

Despite the smoothness of Norah Jones's voice coming out of the speakers, I grip the steering wheel harder. A multilane road similar to this once swept me to work and back, with twenty-minute morning commutes and afternoon crawls that could last an hour. I think about that time in my car, a waiting made bearable by music and the promise of another kind of life. Both job and commute were behind me now, security traded in for the unknowns of graduate school.

I glance back at the green sedan, which now sits parked a car or two behind me in the next lane. I'd planned my escape poorly, driving to the barn during rush hour. But a scant twelve miles away, beyond the dense ribbon of interstate, things start to change. I imagine the light I'll see once I leave the highway, outlining roadside oaks in gold.

I turn east off the freeway. Some cars follow, but most remain in delays that lengthen with the lowering sun. In the rear-view mirror, chrome from a thousand cars quivers like a modern mirage.

Manny lifts each hoof, a moon edged in metal, before I even reach for it. I move around the horse, picking out mud and looking for stray stones. The gelding waits to set down his right hind. I watch him poise his toe and consider arthritis. He's around fourteen years old now, the deep thirties in a horse's life. Under saddle, his ears still flick back and ask to gallop. I wonder if he remembers the blueprint of his racing life before, with strides that spit up homestretch dirt.

Now, he nibbles my offered palm with a rabbit-soft nose. Closing coffee-brown eyes, he droops his lip while I brush his face. A friend bought him after his race days, giving him a second career.

Not wanting to waste time, I reach for my no-frills English saddle, its thin leather molded to my riding position. I fasten the girth to hold both saddle and two pads underneath. Manny starts to put his ears back, warning me not to tighten the saddle too much at first. In the meantime, he lowers his slender head for the bit.

Kirsten waits on Taylor, who marches around the saddling area with decisive steps. I admire his fitness and the deep muscles that make shadows. A leg injury from last year isn't noticeable.

"You must be riding him again," I say.

"For the past couple weeks."

I lead Manny to the mounting block, tighten his girth a few holes, and swing onto his back so we can catch up to Taylor's sweeping walk. We make a circuit of the tree-lined acreage, the horses walking beside one another. Our circles don't take long, and I start to feel guilty about skipping dressage.

At the end of our second circle, Kirsten stares at the dancing grasses beyond the fenced boundaries, and says, "We could go on the new trails."

I follow her glance to fields crowded with trees and flowers. Like me, she isn't sure if we should spend the time. I have things to do at home; she needs to go to work soon. Still, the wind lures us. I turn Manny into it, his tail fanning out behind him. A gust lifts the hair from my face and pulls me toward it, "I'll open the gates."

I slip the chain over the top of the post before we can change our minds. The gate swings free and the two horses walk through it, their mouths foaming a little at this change of direction.

"It isn't mowed yet," Kirsten says, picking her way among the grasses and watching for surprise ruts. Although we have to be careful, I'm glad the mower hasn't found its way here. The horses glide through the blossoms, their tails swooshing behind them like a wake.

Manny buries his nose in the grasses and bites off a tassel when he thinks I'm not looking. Taylor, still leading, arches his neck against the bit and tests Kirsten's light hold. She's steady with him but doesn't let him pull.

"How's your job?" I ask.

Kirsten rolls her eyes a little. "I'm training coworkers who can't spell."

I nod, thinking it has something to do with the handwriting. Most doctors I know scribble, even though Kirsten's handwriting at the barn is always precise. Penmanship is probably the least of her worries given her graveyard shift at the county jail, a place far from these fields.

Whenever a group of us at the barn relax with beers from the mini-fridge, we imagine being pulled over by a Texas patrol car, its driver bored by a night of inactivity. If we were to get arrested, our first stop would be Kirsten's night shift. Considering this possibility, we drink less. It's not just the shame of running into our friend that slows us down, but the stories she tells—the belligerent offender slashed in a bar fight; the local politician out for a night on the town.

"You're a bad nurse," a man brought in for drunken driving tells Kirsten one night, staring at her with wide, bloodshot eyes as his bare feet hang off the exam table. He runs one hand through his dark hair while the other one grips the table.

"My ankle's *broke*." The man gestures to his unblemished bare foot, holding it up in hopes that Kirsten finds some swelling.

Kirsten writes in her chart without looking up, "Your ankle's fine."

"At least gimme some pills."

"Sorry." Kirsten sets her clipboard on the examination room counter and glances at the man's face, which begins to pucker and redden.

The man glares back at her. "You're a crappy nurse, that's why you work this shift."

"Put your shoes on." Kirsten glances through the door window at the guard outside and nods for him to come in. In one motion, the guard opens the door and grasps the man by the arm. His shoes on but untied, the man mumbles under his breath as the guard leads him away. When he's out of sight, Kirsten sets the clipboard down for a moment and sighs, waiting for the next patient.

The horses snort relaxed sighs as they walk through the grasses, their strides lengthening as our reins loosen. We reach a small incline in the open land where the grasses grow shorter, making the ground more visible. Kirsten turns to me, "Want to trot?"

Without much urging, the horses ease up the hill in a steady two-beat rhythm. I keep the reins loose, balancing forward in the saddle and letting Manny find his footing. Taylor swishes his tail but keeps his rhythm even, slowing to a walk once we crest the small hill. I have the urge to go faster, but I know we need to stay sensible for Taylor's sake.

Manny reads my mind and perks his ears forward, lengthening his walk. Kirsten twirls the reins in front of me as she rides, her body melding into Taylor's assertive steps. A swallow dips down over us, and I follow its dive, keeping alert for the hawk I'd seen last summer. The hawk had landed on a fence post ten feet away, her claws grasping the wood and making it hers. Manny and I had waited, a motionless centaur, until the hawk grew bored with us and swept off into the wind.

Along the tree-lined river, the same breeze lifts our horses' manes. Kirsten and I squeeze with our legs; Taylor and Manny spring into a trot. I watch flowers blur into a ribbon of yellow and the river's elms sigh louder in the breeze we've joined.

We cover land in wide swaths until we reach a ridge near the barn. Kirsten and I slow the horses, and they snort and blow. We guide them up the hillside, their hindquarters hefting them along the top of the ridge.

Manny's breathing slows to normal as he walks beside Taylor. He picks his steps with care along the edge. To the left lie the fields we've swept through; to our right is a small pond lined with underbrush. Glancing again, I spot a small, wheat-colored animal crouching near the pond.

"Look, Kirsten." I ease Manny to a halt. Kirsten and Taylor stop just ahead of us. We keep still and watch the animal, a coyote, unfold. His pointed ears perked, he keeps his tail low and trots a few paces beside the water until he fades into the brush.

Kirsten reaches down to pat Taylor on the neck. "I hear them at night, but I've never seen one that close."

We wait a few minutes before letting the horses walk out with no reins. They stride out, relaxed and close to home. A few butterflies, sentries to this other place, flit by as we walk along the riverbed.

We're quiet as we reach the gate that leads back to the barn. We don't hurry to take off the saddles and brush the horses. Kirsten will go to the jail that night for her night shift. I'll return to the city, weaving through darkened roads marked in headlights. Soon, we'll trade black-eyed Susans for inmates, soaring hawks for traffic. We'll leave the wind behind, which stays to bend the flowers and fan the horses' tails, making grasses sigh.

—Gail Folkins

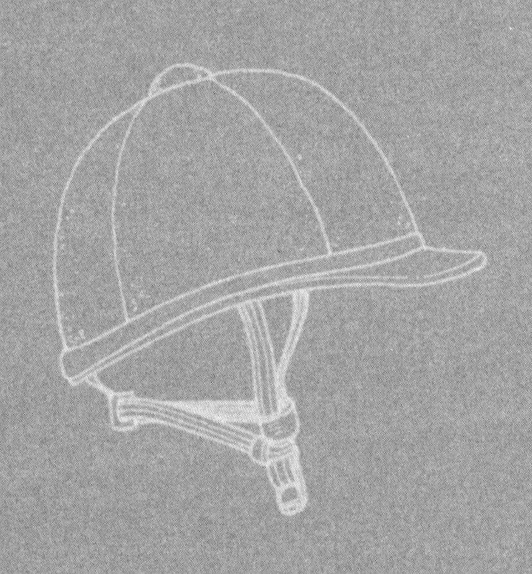

Max the Magnificent

I let out a gasp when I first saw him. He simply took my breath away. As soon as I got home, I called my best friend and gushed, "Oh, Joan, it was love at first sight. My heart started racing, he was so magnificent! What a body! What a gorgeous stud! I was trembling with excitement!"

The painters in my living room stopped what they were doing—I hadn't considered how my description might sound to strangers. And me, a married woman with five children! I put down the phone and turned to the painters.

"I was talking about a horse," I blushed slightly. They nodded respectfully, but I could practically hear the unspoken, "*Sure, lady.*"

I first saw the handsome equine hunk at a lay-up barn. He was recovering from a relatively minor tendon strain, but that wasn't the main reason he was for sale. He hadn't lived up to a pedigree that read like a sure Derby winner: Man O' War, War Admiral, Princequillo, Key to the Mint. These were the legends flowing in Max's veins. But he had no heart for speed.

I offered the owners an embarrassingly small sum for Max (although it was huge to me, it probably seemed like lunch money to the fancy racing folks) with a promise the horse would never show up in a race anywhere. And that's how I came to own Max the Magnificent: a sleek, elegant, black, seventeen-hand, three-year-old stallion. I'd ridden horses all my life but a young Thoroughbred stud? I must have been crazy—and I was—crazy about owning a spectacular horse for once in my life.

Thank heavens my trainer, Kelly Van Vleck, knew how to handle young, green horses. Very quickly, she had Max looking smooth and obedient at the walk, trot, and canter. Looks, however, would turn out to be deceiving once it was time for the owner to get in the saddle.

That October morning had started out cool and crisp. As I eased onto Max's back, I thought I might get too warm in my sweatshirt. With Kelly watching from the rail, I dropped the reins and pulled the sweatshirt up over my head. It didn't occur to me that Max might feel insecure without that contact with the bit, or that he might worry about the sudden movement of arms in the air. I know now that three-year-old Thoroughbreds worry about everything.

The first buck caught me with the sweatshirt stuck on my head. As I tore at the sweatshirt to untangle myself, Max bucked again. He was having a Thoroughbred moment, and I didn't make it any better by waving a red sweatshirt around his ears. "Let go of the sweatshirt!" yelled Kelly.

A horse's antenna are always up, and he is always ready to detect frightening situations. This is how he survives in the wild.

When afraid, a horse runs—unless there is something scary on his back. In that case, he tries to buck it off, and then he runs. That's why I left a snow-angel imprint of my body in the arena. At least the sand was soft.

For nine years Max and I worked on the fear factor—his and mine. If a noise frightened him, and I startled too, he would bolt, spin, or buck. If my hands were tense on the reins, he tensed his body to match.

About halfway into our relationship, a fresh opportunity arose. Max and I were on our own by then, on my own horse property and without Kelly's guidance. Kelly had been my crutch, always there to help me work out the old and new fears. Now I decided to sign up for a "novice cross-country" training clinic taught by a noted expert at a neighbor's stable.

The instructor, Brian Sabo, set up a series of jumps that, once mastered, would improve the confidence level of both horse and rider. All of us in the class did well until Brian raised the height of the oxer three inches. An oxer consists of two parallel jumps from two to five feet apart that the horse should jump as one fence. It didn't seem scary at first, but those few extra inches made the oxer seem gigantic to me. And because of my fear, Max thought that oxer meant the end of his life. Even the spectators were terrified for us. Brian had us pull up.

"Sue, I want you to sing 'Row Your Boat' while you ride." He added, "Don't stop until I like the sound of the song."

Max and I made quite a few passes over the oxer while I screamed the song, staccato and loud, with all the words flung out of my mouth.

Brian said, "Keep going. I don't like the song yet."

Finally, the song began to take on a rhythm and tone more pleasing to the ear. It was more pleasing to Max as well, which was the point. As I relaxed and focused on the song instead of the jump, Max's fear antenna lowered. We jumped the oxer four times with a lovely, rhythmic, and safe cadence. The feeling that I wanted to throw up disappeared. The onlookers applauded.

The song trick stayed with us, especially on trail rides. When Max spooked, he never ran away with me, but on several occasions, he threatened to scare the breeches off me. "Row Your Boat" didn't work as well in those situations, but "Amazing Grace" did the trick. Something about "t'was grace that taught my heart to fear and grace my fears relieved" calmed us both. Max loved that song, and if a horse can smile he did, with his happy hooves cruising down the path.

It took many years for me to fully understand that if I couldn't control my fears, Max couldn't control his. A devastating accident when I was fifty-seven years old drove home the point. I broke my hip in a fall on my back porch. The stress of the surgery ignited a simmering immune disorder. I would heal from the hip fracture, the doctors said, but there was no cure for this strange autoimmune malfunction.

The bone-healing process took a long time. Neighbors pitched in and took care of Max when I could only push a walker from the bed to the bathroom. I missed my horse. We had developed a solid friendship in nine years. He was part of my family, and I loved him dearly. When I was able to get around on crutches, I thought I could manage feeding him, but I couldn't handle another fall. Max sensed my fear and stayed at the other end of the paddock when I arrived with his hay. It made me sad to see him react to my fear; I imagined he didn't understand why his friend didn't want him right by her side.

When the hip healed, I still had to deal with the energy-sapping immune problem. My doctors told me that stress would make my symptoms worse. My wonderful husband told me to quit my high-tension job as a television producer and just play with horses. Change was paramount because of my health, but what would I do now? The future seemed unclear and scary. Max was never going to help reduce my stress level. He would always be Max the Magnificent, and he would always need me to help him deal with his natural Thoroughbred high-spiritedness. The realization that I wasn't able to handle his challenges anymore hit me very hard. I sobbed whenever I thought about selling him. He was my once-in-a-lifetime, spectacular horse. These troubling thoughts dogged me for weeks until an idea occurred to me: If I found a wonderful home for Max, with someone who would enjoy his magnificence, wouldn't that be the best thing for my dear equine friend? A glimmer of positive feeling raised my spirits.

The day I moved out of my grief and into the light of new possibilities, I walked down to the barn and put my crutches aside. I got out all the brushes and curry combs that had always helped Max feel loved and cared for over these many years. I opened the gate and set all the grooming supplies by the hitching post. Max stood across the paddock, quietly following my every move. When I had arranged everything to my satisfaction, I looked over at him but made no move in his direction. I smiled but did not speak. Very calmly and purposefully, Max walked toward me. He gently pressed his head into my chest and closed his eyes. I put my arms around his head, and we stood there for several minutes. I knew what Max was telling me. He was glad I wasn't afraid anymore. He had been worried about me. He had missed me and was happy I was feeling better. And he was saying he loved me. Animals have a rich and precise language few people fully appreciate. But I rely on words, so I told him not to be afraid about the future. Somehow I think he understood.

Max helped teach me about overcoming fear: to stand up to it, to not let it rule me, to face new challenges with confidence or, lacking that, to fake it till you make it. (Singing helps.) But the most important lesson Max taught me about fear is that when you let go of your fear about the future, you get the gift of peace.

Max's new owner loves him as much as I do. She takes him on the show circuit in Nevada and California and some of the shows are near my home. I'll probably cry when I see him, but they will be tears of joy. I always wished I could show him off to the world, but I never had the time or the money. Now Katie gets to fulfill that dream for both of us.

I have a new Paint quarter horse, called My Guy. He's attractive, sturdy, reliable, and calm. Last week I gave him a bath behind my barn where there are no fences. The lead rope slipped from my hand, and he stepped on it close under his chin as he dove to eat some grass. A gasp bubbled in my throat, but I choked it back, trying not to signal my fear. My Guy not only snapped the lead rope but broke the leather halter, too. Max the Magnificent had done a similar thing a few years back and bolted through the neighborhood for an hour before I caught him. My Guy looked at me as if to say, *Well, what are you standing there for? Go get another halter.* And that's what I did. My Guy will never be magnificent, but he is mellow, and that's what I need for the future. When I let go of my fear, I found him.

—SUE PEARSON ATKINSON

Experiencing Murphy

When you're young, people always ask, "What do you want to be when you grow up?" We all had those dreams of becoming a movie star or an astronaut. As a very young girl, I wanted to be a cowgirl. I remembered that dream a few months ago when I came across an old picture of myself wearing my favorite cowgirl hat. Like most people, I grew up and moved on to more sensible goals. I attended college and began a long and comfortable career in the finance world. I felt happy with my life, until it was abruptly and irreversibly changed.

Around my fortieth birthday I was diagnosed with a crippling condition called transverse myelitis, which attacks the central nervous system. It left me an incomplete quadriplegic, and within a few years I was dependent on a power wheelchair to get around. Although I still have use of my upper body, it was affected and now the simplest of tasks can prove extremely challenging.

Once I learned to deal with the losses and adjust to my new life, I looked for an outdoor activity that I could participate in. Before TM, I had started climbing classes; obviously, that was no longer an option. For reasons I didn't understand, none of the well-known activities for the disabled interested me, even though I had enjoyed other sports, like skiing, in the past. So I kept looking.

One evening, I was watching *The Horse Whisperer* when it suddenly came to me: Maybe I could find a place that would teach me how to ride a horse. My decision shocked me, but I was even more stunned by how excited I felt at the prospect. I'd never ridden a horse before, except for one barn-sour Clydesdale I'd clung to for dear life. Horses were beautiful, large, and unpredictable creatures that scared me to death. I also wasn't much of an animal lover—a parakeet was the closest thing I'd had to a pet. But horseback riding felt right. A week later I had found a therapeutic riding facility and was scheduled to start lessons that month.

When I first met with a physical therapist at the Little Bit Therapeutic Riding Center, I expected to talk about my specific needs and decide which horse best suited me. But there was no easing into this process. Within minutes, I was sitting on top of a 1,200-pound horse. The ground looked very far away and with my limited balance I felt very unsteady. Added to that was my fear that this huge animal could turn on me at any minute. With someone leading the horse and a person walking on either side, I managed to stay on as we went around the arena. Despite my white knuckles, when I dismounted, I felt like I was on cloud nine.

I asked my instructor if I could learn to ride independently so I'd look like a real horsewoman.

"You can do whatever you feel capable of," was his reply. I was stunned. I asked the question again to make sure he'd heard me right. He laughed but the answer was the same. For the first time since my diagnosis, I heard a "yes" when it came to achieving physical goals. For the first time since my diagnosis, I was once again given permission to hope and, for the first time, I had some control over my own destiny.

Remembering that moment even now brings tears to my eyes. One of the most difficult adjustments I'd had to make was giving up control and learning how to balance hope with reality. The first few years after the onset of TM, I tried hard to find ways to continue walking and to lead what I thought was a "normal" life, only to feel like a square peg shoved into a round hole. At that time, the only thing left to do was what felt like giving in to the disease. It wasn't until later that I realized I was just learning how to live with it. But now, here I was in a place where I could have a sense of empowerment again, if only for a moment.

It took me a while to get comfortable with horses. After a few mismatches, I began to lose hope and think maybe I wasn't cut out to be a horsewoman after all. It was around this time that I got to know Murphy, and I very unwillingly fell in love.

When I first met Murphy, he was assisting another rider. A Norwegian Fjord, Murphy was an amazingly beautiful and somewhat regal-looking horse, but I had no desire to ride him. As a small draft horse, just over fourteen hands, he didn't fit the cowpony image fixed in my imagination. I wanted to ride a "real" horse. When my instructor suggested I try Murphy, I grudgingly agreed.

The first thing I noticed was that I wasn't nearly as far from the ground as I'd been on the other horses; at least that seemed less dangerous. As I settled into my seat of blankets and surcingle, I realized that Murphy's wider base dramatically improved my balance. I was surprised by how much safer I felt. Maybe the instructor knew what she was doing after all.

Murphy's particular gait also contributed to my sense of security. Although I didn't realize it, his steady and predictable steps reassured me. I don't remember when I became aware of the fact that I wasn't afraid of riding anymore. Each week I looked forward to my next riding lesson, and I began sharing more and more Murphy stories with my coworkers.

Once Murphy's movement had won me over, it was only a matter of time before his personality did the same. From the time I'd arrived at Little Bit, I'd heard stories about how a horse would do some amazing thing to take care of its rider, or adjust to a rider's mood or physical situation. I envied the connection some people seemed to have with the different horses, but I was skeptical. I didn't notice it myself and felt a bit guilty about it.

As my fears diminished while riding Murphy, something else started to happen. Volunteers commented on Murphy's calm demeanor with me compared to his less desirable behavior in earlier classes. I had started taking his good behavior for granted. On trail rides together, he never once succumbed to his temptation for grass. I had heard stories about his reactions to loud noises, but that was not the calm, collected horse I knew. I'd even seen him drag unsuspecting volunteers into stalls looking for dinner when he was supposed to be heading to the arena. But when I led him from the barn to the paddocks at night, he not only walked calmly with me, but waited patiently for my wheelchair to muck through the mud. Although I was aware of his different behavior with me, and I was growing fonder of him, I still wasn't convinced there was a connection—until the day of the parade.

Murphy was selected to pull a cart in a small local parade. The event was exhausting for him but he made it through without too much fuss. Unfortunately, he was needed in several classes afterwards so he wasn't able to take much of a break. I felt bad for how hard he had to work, so I went into his stall to offer him some comfort. I rested my head against his shoulder and talked to him, and he seemed to relax. But it wasn't until my lesson later that day that I found out what a difference I made in his life. Murphy was his usual mellow self in my class. What I didn't know was that after the parade he had been so wound up that he had bitten a volunteer. At that moment, I finally understood what the others had been trying to tell me. From the day I started riding him, Murphy was making a special effort to take care of me. From then on Murphy was no longer just a horse, he was my best friend.

I feel proud and privileged that Murphy accepted me into his "inner circle." The special bond between us has taught me to love and trust him implicitly. He recognizes the sound of my wheels before I even get to his stall and waits expectantly at the gate. I try hard to listen to his needs, as he does to mine. He was a great comfort to me the year both my mother and best friend were diagnosed with breast cancer.

Getting to know Murphy has opened a world of emotional connections with animals and people, and taught me a lot about myself. He has shown me a place of unconditional love, understanding, and trust. My physical condition ended my corporate career, but I now spend a great deal of time with animals. I volunteer at a children's hospital and have started writing again. In many ways I'm happier now than I've ever been, despite the challenges each day presents.

These days I need to ride a horse trained in neck reining, so I no longer ride Murphy regularly. He has given me the courage to continue working toward my goal of riding independently. To my great satisfaction, I've started walking my horse independently in controlled circumstances and trotting without a leader. In 2004, I competed in my first show for disabled riders and came home with a first-place ribbon in a walk-only equitation class.

Murphy has been on his best behavior and has become the star of the barn. The staff came to realize that, while he loved his job at Little Bit, he needed to be challenged occasionally, so now he also assists independent riders. In 2002, he won the Horse of the Year award from the North American Riding for the Handicapped Association for his outstanding service. I visit him every week and consider him my best equine friend.

Riding and connecting with horses continue to strengthen me physically and emotionally, and give me the courage and the heart to enjoy every single day. I once read, "Dreams are not out there in the stars somewhere, they're right here in our hearts." Thanks to Murphy, I get to live out my cowgirl dream after all. It just turned out to be a little different and far more rewarding than I had imagined. My hope is that everybody can experience a Murphy at some time in their lives.

—SUSAN HUTCHINSON

Galloping into Forty

Three days before my fortieth birthday, my boyfriend of six years took me out to dinner. Over a glass of our favorite pinot noir, he whispered, "When you get home tonight, pack your bags. I'm flying you to Amelia Island."

Richard knew I was less than thrilled about officially entering middle age. He also knew there were two things I dreamed of that I'd not yet attained: riding a horse on the beach, and becoming a published author.

There was little he could do about the latter, but as a computer nerd and pilot, he had the skills to research the few beaches that still allowed horseback riding, and fly us there in a rented single-engine Cessna. At last, I would fulfill a long-held fantasy of riding the most glorious creature on land along the very edge of the earth.

Thirty years ago, as a horse-crazy kid, I was shocked when my mother got a horse for her fortieth birthday. I'd been collecting plastic Breyer horses and decorating my room with horse posters and drawings for years.

"But *I'm* the one who loves horses!" I cried. "Why does *Mom* get one?"

My father calmly explained that my mother didn't collect posters and models, but she had loved horses all her life, and this was what she wanted more than anything. He also said that if I was nice instead of jealous, I might get to help take care of this big buckskin addition to the family.

After months of proving that I was serious, and more than willing to help with even the most mundane aspects of horse care, my mother hired an instructor to give me riding lessons. I rode every chance I got until the day I went away to college.

It had been a long time since then, and I was not sure I could still ride like I had in my teens. I'd outgrown the posters and statues, but I still loved horses just as much as my mother probably did when she was facing forty.

After a thrilling and scenic flight, Richard landed our little plane on the narrow runway in the middle of the island. We took a cab to Elizabeth Pointe, a luxury bed and breakfast, where we stayed in a sun-filled room with fluttering linen curtains whispering with ocean breezes.

We rode bikes around the island the first day, then slow, plodding horses along a trail to the beach the second day. It was a horseback ride to be sure, and Richard was a trouper to come along, but he knew this was not the ride I'd hoped and longed for all these years.

On the third day, we walked around the historic district and looked at antiques. The evening before we left, Richard talked a local woman who owned racehorses into taking me out for a real ride. Debbie would trailer her horses to meet us on a deserted stretch of beach, and then drop me off at the airport after the ride.

The morning I turned forty, we woke at dawn and had breakfast on the rocking chair porch, watching the interplay between waves and seagulls. When we got to the beach, Debbie was right where she said she'd be, unloading two stunning and lively horses. She turned to greet me, gloved hand outstretched.

"So, Kim, you ready for the ride of a lifetime?"

Debbie was tall, lanky, and blonde, with a sort of sideways rough-and-ready-for-anything smile. She introduced me to Sandman, her tall white Thoroughbred, and then to the younger of the two, a sleek, leggy chestnut with a white stripe down his nose. "This is Taco," she said. "And other than carrots, the thing he loves most in life is a full-out gallop. Think you can you handle him?"

I looked out at the waves, my hair whipping in the wind. "I'd sure like to try," I said.

She nodded and handed me a slim English saddle. "Let me see you up on him," she said with a wink. "A rider's seat tells me all I need to know."

I let Taco sniff the back of my hand, and he took a deep heavy breath, and threw his head twice in greeting. Once I had settled the light saddle onto his back and guided the gentle snaffle bit into his mouth, Debbie offered me a leg up. There I sat, my head in the trade winds, 1,200 pounds of glorious horse beneath me.

"Nice," said Debbie. "Deep in the saddle, heels down, head up. You're good to go."

We started off slowly, Taco in front at a brisk walk, his mane swinging in rhythm, the hum of the surf in my ears. The friendly nod of Taco's chiseled head made me smile: We were moving in time with the tides, and all the earth made sense from horseback. The view framed between his alert ears made the gray and green of the beach all the more beautiful. It was as if he was telling me, *Look, here—out there—this is the world.*

Behind me the rush and roar of the ocean carried Debbie's words away as Taco picked up speed, a bouncing trot followed by the rocking magic of a canter. There was a swooshing of the sand and surf, then a moment later, his Thoroughbred muscles kicked in and the clouds began to blur, the earth echoing under his thundering pace.

Taco was pedal-to-the-metal, and my heart raced. When he swerved to miss some foam riding in on a big wave, I lost a stirrup. I thought I was a goner. How was I ever going to get it back at this speed?

I looked back at Debbie smiling and laughing a good fifty feet behind us. I glanced down at my flailing stirrup and Taco's blur of legs against the sand and wondered if I should attempt the emergency dismount I'd learned at fourteen. Could I dive past those sharp hooves and roll on such hard sand? Moments later, I was thanking the good heavens and gods of horseflesh because Taco slowed and pulled up, allowing Sandman to catch up with us.

"This is where we turn around," said Debbie, breathing hard. "Race you back?"

Richard had made my fortieth birthday a very happy one indeed. I'd eaten a Captain Van's shrimp burger in a giant oak tree, pedaled a bike all over an island, walked down to the beach alone to sit surrounded by seagulls, and stood in the surf as I regained my bearings with the earth, feeling gravity's pull. There was that moment when I turned in my saddle to see a smiling Rich on a slow brown pony at the end of the line, and then that last taste of salty ocean air on my face while tearing through the surf on a leggy chestnut steed.

So few events in this life measure up to the gems of dreams we hold and turn over in our minds. The more we long for a moment, a thing, a chance at that fleeting image, the less likely it becomes that the reality can ever match our vision.

This was one day in my life that exceeded the fantasy—echelons above and miles beyond the small romantic notion of clopping along the beach on a horse "one day." This had been a race with the earth, an awakening of my heart. This was holding my life up for an ageless glimmering instant of joy. Yes, I still turned forty, but that day on the beach I was sure that on Taco the racehorse, I could outrun time and the wind eternal.

While I waited for Rich to prepare the plane for our trip back home, I took an arm's-length picture of myself before that bold, glowing grin could wear off. I wanted to remember this moment of deep and total happiness. I'll always cherish that picture of me the day I galloped into forty on horseback.

Waiting for me at home, I found a letter from a well-known literary magazine asking for permission to publish a story submitted months earlier. It was the most delicious icing possible on top of the very best of birthday cakes.

—Kimberley Freeman

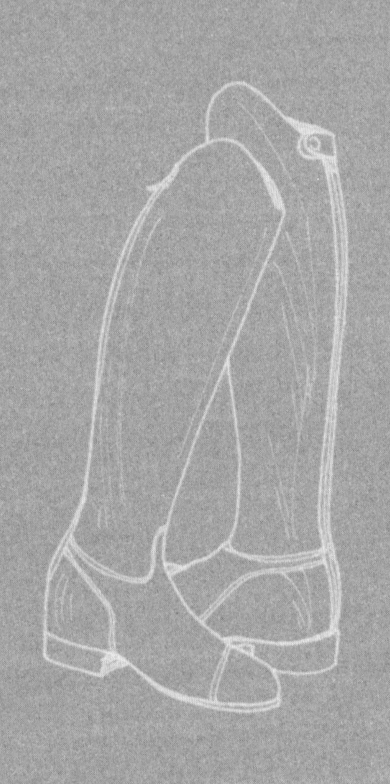

It's Only a Paper Horse

When my daughter Olivia first started drawing horses, she was two years old. At the end of each week a pile of papers would come home from day care covered with horses running, horses leaping, horses dipping their heads, each centered on a plain white background. Their accuracy was a little freakish.

"How do you explain this?" my husband, Tom, would ask. He held a chalk rendering, just a few deft strokes conveying not only the form but the movement, the very nature, of that day's horse. I could only shrug my shoulders, no better able to account for our daughter's talent than he.

Where had it come from? Not from Tom or me, that much was obvious. Olivia had given up asking me to "make a horse, Mommy" after two or three miserably failed attempts that looked vaguely like llamas. Tom's sketching abilities were limited to the creation of a single cartoon fish, which he drew over and over in a vain attempt to be useful. Granted, Olivia had two artistic relatives: her paternal great-grandfather, an architect and artist, who produced a painting a day until he was ninety-five years old; and her maternal grandfather, a weekend doodler who wowed the neighborhood with life-sized copies of Disney characters for pin-the-bow-on-Cinderella games at his daughters' childhood birthday parties. But looking to ancestors twice and three times removed seemed a bit of a reach.

The provenance of Olivia's ability was not the only mystery. There was the question of her chosen subject matter, since we lived in Manhattan, not Montana. Olivia was drawing something she saw inside her head, not outside her window, given that the window of the day care center in question was on the ground floor of a Midtown skyscraper.

It was a little hard to know what to do with this development, so in typical yuppie fashion, Tom and I enrolled her in an afterschool program for young artists. Olivia resisted. "I don't need anyone to show me how to draw!" she shouted, plainly offended.

I could hardly disagree with her. As the years went by, Olivia worked harder and more successfully on her horses than I had seen anyone work at anything, ever. She produced from ten to thirty drawings a day. Sitting on the floor at our glass coffee table, half-watching afternoon cartoon shows, she would pull out a packet of white printer paper and start with a few lines, and then put the page aside, dissatisfied. She looked like a filly herself: pale blonde hair like a mane down her back, long stick-like arms and legs coming out of her short, round trunk. On the next page, she'd make a change, then another. Not quite right. On the third page, she'd alter the way she inclined the horse's head, or the proportions of its body, or the lines of its mane. No good. By the tenth page, she'd have gotten the look she wanted, call for Mommy, and hand the page to me without looking up, already starting on Horse the Next. There in my hand would be an image of pure movement and beauty, acute and descriptive. And nowhere in the room was there an image of a horse to be used for reference. Since we had remained contented city dwellers—now in San Francisco—there were still no horses in her daily life, either. There seemed to be no other way to nurture her art but to change that.

This was no easy task. In any direction, there were bridges and punishing commutes between us and any flesh-and-blood horses I could find. My first effort found a lakeside, all-outdoor camp in the East Bay for a whopping $650 a week; we choked down the bills for one summer before admitting it would have to be our last. The next year we spent some time in the Berkshire Hills of Massachusetts, where my in-laws have a country home. A nearby YMCA camp incorporated a lesson or two a week into its schedule. Olivia reported that she'd rather spend no time at all in the presence of real horses than have her appetite for their company stoked but not satisfied by a mere ninety minutes a week. The next summer we scored a spot in the San Francisco YMCA's one-week horse camp—so affordable and popular that admission is by lottery—but we couldn't get in the next year and our live-horse issue persisted.

With horses solidly restricted to her fantasy life, Olivia branched out to unicorns, then, at nine, began cartooning, with Japanese animé as her jumping-off point. I noticed that she had ceased representational drawing entirely, never having practiced humans at all. Only horses received that kind of attention. As for people, they had oversized, square-shaped eyes with enormous pupils and round faces, or eyes that were nothing more than a vertical line, all expression coming from the tilt of the brows above.

"Don't you want to learn how to draw a realistic face?" I asked her hopefully, knowing better than to tell her about the latest life-drawing class I had seen advertised in *Bay Area Parent* magazine.

"No," Olivia said neutrally, concentrating on the sweeping strokes of yet another horse's windblown mane and tail.

Another day I found a story in the *New York Times* about a sketch artist who was making a big splash at galleries with her elegant pencil portraits. "Check this out, Olivia," I said, tearing out the story and handing it to her. "I bet you could draw a face like this one."

She looked at it quizzically, and then sat on the floor in front of her ever-present pile of printer paper. Six tries later, she handed me her final effort, her eyes full of anger.

"I can't do it," she spat. I looked at the page. Olivia had attempted to copy one of the drawings in the article.

"Why don't you try to draw a picture of yourself, or me, or Daddy? We'd love to have one."

"I can only make horses look real!" she said.

"But that's because you practice horses so much. If you practiced making portraits of people you'd be just as good at them."

"But I don't *want* to draw people. I want to draw horses." She sat back down to start in on yet another long, star-graced nose.

The first week of fourth grade, Olivia was chosen as the year's inaugural class VIP, a privilege all fourth graders enjoy during the course of the year. VIPs are school stars for the week, culminating on an especially delicious Friday when they get to leave their school uniforms at home and wear street clothes to make a presentation to the entire school about their greatest passion.

"That's easy," I said to her when we sat down to prepare her speech. "You can talk about how much you love to draw."

Olivia rolled her blue-green eyes as if she couldn't imagine how she could have come from a mother so dense.

"Drawing isn't my passion, Mom," she said. "It's horses!" Whereupon she bagged up an assortment of plastic Breyer horses, china unicorns, stuffed ponies, and a folder that contained—yes, one pencil sketch—and toted it to school. There, she spoke eloquently about all things equine as if we lived on a ranch.

Sitting in a VIP-parent chair at the back of the room, I watched Olivia and thought about the difference between the dreams she had and the ones I had for her. Visions of Paris salons and Pixar Animation cubicles danced in my head, while *she* fantasized about tack. As Olivia stood before the whole school, she held up an eight-by-ten-inch photo she had taken in Kenya on a summer safari with her grandparents. *There you go!* I thought with great satisfaction. *At least she got off the subject long enough to talk about her big trip.* But then I realized that the picture she had insisted on enlarging was of—what else?—a zebra, the horse of the African savannah. She put the photo down and pulled the pencil drawing out of her folder, holding it at arm's length in two hands and rotating her body slowly from one side of the room to the other so each member of the audience could see. An audible "Oooh" rose from the cross-legged children on the floor in front of her. I noticed that this horse, unlike most of the others before it, wasn't drawn in a void. There were grasses under its feet along with a rock it was leaping, and clouds in the far distance. This horse had a sense of place, a physical context. It occurred to me that whether art had awakened her interest in horses or horses had awakened her interest in art didn't really matter. What mattered was the awakening.

—STEPHANIE LOSEE

Something about Mollie

Mollie lost the sight in her left eye long before I knew her. During a winter storm, when the wind was hurling objects around the ranch where she lived, a piece of metal roof tore loose and hit her in the eye as she stood in her stall. For months afterward her owner, Steve, tried to save her sight with eye drops and a patch but his efforts failed. She must have been in a lot of pain because she stopped eating and her weight sloughed off her like dead skin. She startled at anything on her left side. No longer was she the horse who would calmly take Steve to the drive-through window at McDonald's.

My becoming Mollie's owner was as much of an accident as her eye injury. A girlfriend had invited me to dinner where Steve was one of the guests. As conversation flowed after the meal, Steve started talking about how great his horse was. My ears perked up. I was still recovering mentally from a bad fall off my previous horse, a fall that had broken both legs and an arm. I had given that horse away because I never felt safe on him again. Most people would have abandoned horseback riding after that, but I was a dyed-in-the-wool horse lover.

Steve sensed that I might be interested. He cornered me in the kitchen and gave me the hard sell. "Mollie's a registered Arab. She's beautiful and willing to please." I couldn't help myself—I listened.

"But there's just one thing you should know about her," he went on. "She's blind in one eye."

"What?"

Steve hurried on. "She's totally adjusted to it. You'd never know the difference. So, do you want to take a look at her? She'd be perfect for you. I really don't have time for two horses anymore."

So I get the half blind one?

I don't know why, but I went to see her. Steve was right. She was a beautiful bay with a long black mane and tail and a face like a fawn's. She was as sweet as a cookie. But that blind eye. It was milky blue with a white disk in the center. Would she be okay to ride? I decided to lease her.

We got off to a good start. Steve introduced me to a trainer, and I began my first dressage lessons. Mollie's abilities surpassed mine. She could do a flying lead change and a pirouette at the canter; in fact, cantering was her favorite gait. Trail riding was a different story. Starting out, Mollie had to examine everything on the right side of the trail with her good eye. Once we turned in the direction of home, she wanted to gallop back to the barn. I had to struggle with her as she pranced sideways. It was unsettling for someone who had survived a whopper of an accident out on the trail. I decided to stick to the arena.

Despite her challenging behavior, Mollie had a magnetism that I wanted in my life. She was always thrilled to see me when

I arrived at the ranch. The comedy routine at bath time had her grinning toothily as I sprayed water into her mouth. And when I rode her in the arena, she seemed to know what I was going to ask her to do. Perhaps her partial blindness had developed her intuition. I decided to stop leasing her and buy her.

One day I noticed a change in her blind eye. It was larger than the right eye, and a clear liquid drained from the duct. The vet looked at it, but said an equine ophthalmologist needed to examine her. That was easier said than done. My vet didn't know one, so I combed the Yellow Pages and the Internet. I finally found Dr. Silverman, who was relatively nearby and willing to come to the ranch. There was one condition, however: In order to examine her eye, it had to be dark, just like when we have our eyes examined. Since Mollie was outside, Dr. Silverman was going to have to come at night.

I felt like Dr. Watson helping Sherlock Holmes as I helped Dr. Silverman set up the slit lamp and the biomicroscope in the dark. I peered into the cavernous depths of Mollie's eye looking for clues to the condition of her eyesight. Of course, the doctor's trained eye could see far more than I could. After the exam, he explained that the damage had resulted in glaucoma, a buildup of fluid behind the eye, and the pressure from the fluid probably felt like a constant throbbing headache to Mollie.

"You have two options," he said. "Medicate her eye with glaucoma drops three times a day for the rest of her life, or have the eye removed and a prosthesis put in."

"What would the prosthesis look like?"

"Like a ball in the eye socket covered over with skin."

He told me that a glass eye would be very expensive, but even the prosthesis would cost a thousand dollars. I groaned.

I had just been laid off from my job, so a glass eye was out of the question. So was medicating her eye three times a day while I was looking for work full-time. I couldn't afford to pay someone to do it for me, either, so the prosthesis seemed to be the only answer. But how was I going to pay for it? I went home that night very discouraged.

My boyfriend had an idea. "Why don't you ask the newspaper if they would print a notice asking for donations toward Mollie's surgery?"

The newspaper was more than willing. They not only printed a half-page story about Mollie, but they also sent a photographer to take her picture. All the newspaper asked in return was that a reputable third party collect the donations. A fellow horse owner suggested Actors and Others for Animals.

As soon as the article appeared, the donations started coming in. The response amazed even the folks at Actors and Others for Animals. Soon there was more than enough money to cover the surgery. When people refused to take back the excess donations, the organization used the money to help other animals in need.

Mollie had her surgery at the best horse hospital in the area. She came home the next day, slightly bruised and swollen where her eye had been. She was the same horse, but now she was a celebrity at the ranch. Everybody wanted to give her a carrot and Mollie didn't refuse a single one.

Things are back to normal now. Mollie and I continue our dressage lessons. She patiently waits for me to get as good at it as she is. Sometimes we go out on the trail, when it's not too windy, after I've lunged all the excess energy out of her. She prefers to have another horse along on her left side. And people at the ranch still go out of their way to visit her.

Clearly, there's something about Mollie.

—Wendy Beth Baker

Left in the Lust

For a horsewoman to find herself middle-aged is no small thing. Yesterday I was sixteen and praying I'd find a handsome boyfriend who would give me things and let me wear a Barbie wedding dress on my special day. At a recent Native American powwow, I was dismayed to discover that I could no more mount the mechanical bull than I could play middle linebacker for the Dallas Cowboys. I have not been a happy camper since. In my head, I was limber and grinning as the bull flung my flexible young body around; in my head, I made an Olympic-quality dismount and landed with arms spread. My body, meanwhile, was looking for a seat in the shade where I could suck down my ice cream while younger bodies wobbled and shrieked on the back of the machine.

Be that as it may, this middle-aged thing bears closer scrutiny. What am I in the middle of? Middle of the road? Middleweight? Certainly not middle of my life. I'm sure I've not come halfway through in such a short time as this. (I still haven't worked up the nerve to tell my dad I don't think he looks good in plaid trousers.) It only took one pretty little mare to show me my place. She was standing in my field, a Thoroughbred with gaits like silk and the conformation of a calendar horse. Dolly was my daughter's horse, and she was for sale. My daughter, twenty-five and soon to be married, was far wiser than I; she recognized she needed to cut down on the excitement in her life and take a more realistic approach. She talked at length about the "packer" she would buy with the proceeds from the pretty mare's sale. I, much older and therefore not nearly so wise, lusted after that mare. I want to be the one slipping lithely onto her back, riding those amazing, silky strides, and jumping with flair and abandon. My daughter offered me the horse for below her public asking price, which rendered the mare quite inexpensive compared to other horses with less talent and coarser looks.

Wallowing in my newfound stigma of "middle age," I could take it no more. Checkbook in hand, I strode confidently to the barn and asked my daughter's permission to ride the mare.

Dolly was a wonderful horse in many ways, absolutely sane from the ground. I could do whatever I wished to her, around her, above and below her, and she would stand without moving. She loved to be scratched and have her udder rubbed, and would stand ground-tied outside the tack room door waiting for cookies at the end of a ride. She hated to be caught in the main pasture, but in a smaller area she came when called. I brushed and polished and hugged and fussed over her until we both sighed with pleasure. I tacked her up, and off we went to the ring.

I'd ridden Dolly many times before, but not recently—certainly not since middle age had found me. While Jess was at college, I had even taken the mare to the back field under Western tack and run barrels with her. I had great faith that she would remember me with fondness and give me the wonderful, electric—but safe—ride I craved.

Maybe it was my imagination, but when my butt hit the saddle and Dolly began to tap dance, she seemed a bit *too* electric. As we walked around the ring, calm replaced my initial skepticism as she stretched her neck and back and sighed. I smiled. She snorted. I put some leg on her and urged her into a lovely extended trot. She obliged.

By this time, Jess was watching; her little Morgan, the Rat, grazed at the end of a lead. She shouted a couple of instructions, which I followed. Dolly got rounder and more collected, and my heart sang.

"Push her into the canter," Jess called. "Slow and easy; don't squeeze. Just think 'canter' and she'll go."

Before the thought had even budded in my brain, Dolly caught it and ran with it. She wasn't running away, she was just cantering, those athletic, balanced strides I so envied unrolling under me. I should have had a nirvana moment at that point, but I didn't. Dolly reached the corner before I was balanced for the turn. She didn't dump me, but she was listing to the left, and I was hanging onto her mane with one hand, trying not to lean with her and knock her down.

A few strides later, I brought her to a trot, then a walk, and at last I breathed. What was that all about? Where was my leg? How could I have reached the terror threshold so quickly when all we were doing was cantering along the familiar fence line? This, I concluded, was middle age pounding me between the shoulder blades and saying, "Welcome to the downhill slide!"

The question became, then, where would I go with this? I could buy the beautiful mare and hope that eventually my heart would sink back down out of my throat to its proper spot in my chest, or I could admit that perhaps my young Paint gelding was challenge enough at this stage of my life. I chose the latter.

I'm better now. It's taken months of visits to the gym for me to jam my body back into some sort of condition for riding. I had gotten lazy and cocky. It had been two years since my last challenging ride, and it showed. Forty-plus years in the saddle does not a rider make. The lust remains, but it is tempered by a certainty that I can no longer push the envelope. Hell, I'm lucky if I can muster enough spit to glue it shut. I've still got horses to ride, and there are exciting moments, but I'm content to watch from the sidelines as other, extraordinarily limber, young dressage-queens-in-training come to try the pretty mare's flowing gaits.

I'll pack my aging quarter horse into the trailer and head to my trainer's for another lesson, and I'll be as stiff and sore as I need to be after an hour of "bring that shoulder *up,* not *out!*" Like the bodies waving from the back of the mechanical bull and the handsome young men waiting to catch them when they fall, pretty Dolly will take her place on the Who Are You Kidding list. We'll both be better off that way.

—JOANNE M. FRIEDMAN

Thunder Rescued Me

Equestrians say that your first horse is like your first love. I met mine on a chilly October day. For months my friend Scott had been trying to find a horse for me. He knew that I only had $200 to spend.

Scott called early that morning, "Reba, I've found a rescue horse, cheap. He's at the barn. Come take a look."

My stomach did somersaults as I raced through the morning traffic. It was as if Santa had arrived early. Through the eyes of a child, I gazed at the blue roan gelding running circles in the round pen, first in one direction, then the other. *What are you doing, boy? Searching for an escape?*

At fifteen hands and half starved, he wasn't quite the beauty I'd envisioned. His bones poked through his skin like a malnourished child's. His blue-gray hair was matted into ringlets, and raw welts striped his hind legs.

"He looks rough, but with a little doctoring and a couple hundred pounds on him, he'll make a nice horse." Scott said. "The calmness of the quarter horse should make up for the skittishness of the Arabian in him."

I studied the horse. His wild eyes stared back at me, sizing me up, too. I reached my hand toward him, but he jerked his head away from me. Sweat beaded on my forehead. Maybe I was making a mistake. "Tell me more about him."

Scott grinned. He knew I was hooked. "He was abused pretty badly. His owner was a drunk, known for mistreating his animals. Some people said he would tie his horses to a tree for days to break their spirit." Scott leaned against the round pen. "On a trail ride last week, he rode him across railroad tracks, and they fell. The horse was hung on the tracks with a train approaching in the distance."

I shivered. Scott frowned. "The owner and his buddy couldn't get him up, and he opened a knife to cut the horse's throat. They finally freed him, just in time."

Poor baby. He had been through hell. Scabbed-over wounds, bare patches, and fresh scars that revealed thickened flesh and jagged hair lines—those were just the visible injuries. The emotional ones would take much longer to heal, I knew. The past year had taught me that fact. This horse needed someone with patience and time. He needed stability, daily training, and an experienced horseperson. I was an emotional mess myself and could offer none of those things.

Even my riding lessons had been filled with turmoil. My instructor had yelled at me constantly. Most days I left in tears, confused over why I was putting myself through the ordeal. But I was not a quitter, and a voice inside me said, *Do not give up.* Had Thunder's abusive owner broken his spirit just as unfortunate events had almost broken mine?

I know how he feels. This had been the worst year of my life. At thirty-eight, I had left my dream home and finalized my divorce. My children were hurt and confused. On top of it all, I had lost my job. Standing up for my beliefs had cost me my confidence and my security.

Thoughts raced through my head faster than I could sort them. This horse had been traumatized. Were we really so different? We were both wounded and afraid to trust again. The only thing I had to offer was unconditional love. Would it be enough? How could I rescue him when I needed rescuing myself?

At least you have your self-respect, friends had reminded me. Unfortunately, self-respect doesn't pay the bills. The question of bills raised another issue: How could I justify spending money on a horse? I had already rescued so many dogs and cats that my house looked like an animal shelter. Everyone thought I had lost my mind, including my very practical mother.

My riding instructor's words hammered home my doubt: "It's all about balance." Maybe I *was* off balance.

I had read that many Native Americans believe that each animal has something to teach us and that we are drawn to certain animals because of something that we lack. Horses teach us balance. It fit.

I closed my eyes. I felt a slight nudge and opened my eyes. The blue roan had padded over to me. He nickered, pawed the ground, and dropped his head. His cold nose brushed my shoulder as he sniffed my hair. My heart fluttered. Something sweet and fragrant blew in the wind. The sun slipped from behind the clouds and glinted off the gray specks on his coat. He allowed me to pat him and warmth spread through my body. In that moment I felt a kindred spirit with the magnificent lonely beast.

I made my decision. "Whatever happens next, we'll face it together," I whispered. "I love you, buddy."

"How much?" I asked nervously.

Scott grinned. "I'll sell him to you for what I have in him, and if he doesn't work out, I'll buy him back." He removed his Stetson and wiped his brow. "You can keep him here. You pay for feed and hay, and clean the stall."

I reached for my wallet. "With his stormy past, I'll call him Thunder."

Scott took the money and handed me the lead rope. I squealed with delight. I felt ten years old. I owned a horse! He might have been a bag of bones to someone else, but to me he was perfect. I was in love.

I might as well have stayed at the barn that night for all the sleep I got. I lay in bed with schoolgirl dreams of adventures on horseback, white knights, and morning glories surrounding Thunder and me as we cantered to the rhythm of laughter. Happy dreams for a change.

At five the next morning, I gave up on sleep, started the coffee, and climbed into my riding clothes. For the first time in months, I was anxious to see the sunrise. I reached for my boots and laughed aloud when I remembered my first riding lesson. My instructor's unkempt gray hair, rotund waist, and skin-tight leggings had made an unforgettable impression on me. I made quite an impression on her, too. Excited to begin my new adventure, I had bought new Justin boots, a denim shirt sporting a horse logo, and brand-new Wrangler jeans. With arms folded, she smirked as

I waded through the creek in my new designer duds to catch the horse. I remembered my embarrassment that day and vowed today would be better. Thunder needed me.

I was the first to arrive at the stable that morning. The smell of the horses and other farm animals filled my senses, and I felt nostalgia for a carefree childhood with my twin sister. I was anxious to tell her about my new love. She, more than anyone, would understand.

I peered over the stall door, almost expecting it to be empty. Had yesterday been an illusion? But there stood Thunder, damaged and wary, but all mine, calmly nibbling his hay. At the creaking of the door, his head met mine, and we almost collided in our curiosity. I cracked open the stall door and stepped inside. I waited for him to make the first move. He edged toward me cautiously, sniffing and wavering. Then he bowed his head, and his nose brushed my cheek, a sign of trust. My heart soared.

It would be slow, but I was encouraged. We spent the morning hanging out together. I fetched the grooming brushes. Thunder's mane was so tangled that I considered cutting it short. After two frustrating hours of combing and unweaving the knots, I was glad that I hadn't. His long mane was stunning, streaked with black, gray, and white.

I desperately wanted to clip his ears and bridle path but decided to wait, as Thunder continued to shy away from my hand.

Go slowly. Think of him as one of your trauma patients. I talked quietly and explained everything as I did it. By the time Scott arrived, I had Thunder brushed and haltered and was leading him around the barn. I hadn't yet tried to mount him.

My fears proved unfounded; he responded to the saddle like it was part of him. As Scott held the bridle, and I hoisted myself up, I felt like a child trying on new Buster Brown shoes for school. My heart tingled with excitement and pride. I wondered if Thunder was as nervous as I was.

Easy. Slow. I nudged him, "Let's go." To my delight, he cooperated without hesitation in our tentative jaunt inside the round pen.

"Good boy." I stroked his long neck and sighed with relief. After a few rounds, I dismounted and rewarded him with an apple from home. He thanked me by slurping the juice all over my tee shirt. Our love affair had begun in earnest.

Friday night became date night: the barn my sanctuary, Thunder my confidant. He accepted me and taught me to accept myself. Soon, my life began to turn around. Optimism replaced my lingering despair. New life breathed inside me as the bitterness of the past year dissipated. In time, I noticed the flowers blooming, the smell of fresh rain, and the wind on my face. I was filled with an inner peace that had been missing for a long time. Thunder, not my riding instructor, taught me the importance of balance. He carried me when I was too weary to travel on my own, bringing me out of my deep depression into a world filled with enthusiasm and hope. Many times at the end of a ride, he would lower his head and give me an affectionate nudge as if to say, *Thanks for giving me a home.* Thunder's spirit renewed my own.

Thunder changed, too. Soon a silky, shiny coat covered his muscled body. No longer scared or nervous, he was now a confident, reliable, and courageous horse. Together, we spent hours exploring mountain trails. With gentle coaxing and an affirming touch, I taught him to overcome his fear of trains. He would cross the tracks and stay calm at the clatter of an approaching train. Eventually my children joined us and riding together became a healing process for my family.

I remained the only one who could catch Thunder in the open pasture. He was my first horse and one of the greatest loves of my life. My friends say, "You did a noble thing when you rescued that horse."

"You've got it backwards," I reply. "Thunder rescued me."

—Reba Ellen Logan

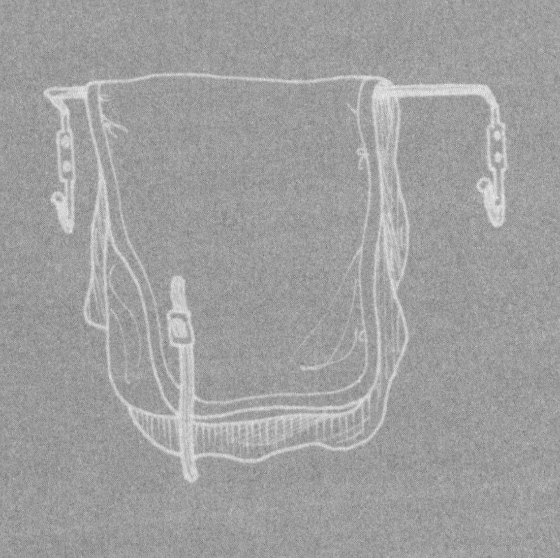

Going Solo

The only reason I signed up for horseback riding lessons in the first place was because my painfully cute younger boyfriend dumped me. I was thirty-one; he was twenty-two. What had started out making me feel years younger had ended with the sudden perception that somehow I'd aged ten years overnight.

"I hate everybody," I announced after the humiliating reality set in.

"Maybe this is a good time to take up a new hobby," one of my friends suggested.

That sounded too much to me like something you'd read in a women's magazine: "Take yourself to the movies! You don't need a man to have fun! Men will fall all over you if you have the self-confidence to go out alone! Then you'll get that man you don't need!"

"I'd rather sit around and hate people," I grumped to my friend.

Still, the novelty of sitting home angrily alone eventually wore off. The ad for a three-week horseback riding class at a local college caught my eye, mainly because it was one of two summer classes that didn't involve swing dancing or screenwriting. I'd never been up close to a horse before, but I imagined it couldn't be any worse than the beast who had just rejected me. I headed to my first session on a warm evening in early July.

"Get here early!" shouted our teacher, even though we'd all gotten there well before class started. Roberta had introduced herself to our small group moments before, launching into the do's and don'ts of horse etiquette. She had the bearing of an army sergeant and the sort of choppy haircut that I associated with women in the military. In her dusty cowboy boots and button-down shirt tucked neatly into skin-hugging riding pants, she was easily over six feet tall. She wasn't heavy, but solid in a way that made me want to shout, "Yes, sir!" to all her directions.

"Drive *exactly* five miles per hour when you're on the property. Stand on the left side of your horse *only*. And *never* punch your horse in the jaw or kick him in the stomach!"

I looked around in surprise. Did we seem like the types to get into bar fights with horses unless expressly forbidden to do so?

"We don't train horses by hitting them; it's wrong and unnecessary. All your horse cares about is, *Mommy, do you love me?* and *Daddy, did I do it right?*" This was good news to me. I'd gotten a little nervous on the way over (don't people sometimes get thrown off these things?), and I liked the idea that my horse might be more unsure of himself than I was.

As we followed Roberta into the large and smelly barn, she resumed her lecture. "Horses are temperamental just like us, and they respond to individuals. If she has a bad ride," Roberta pointed to one of my classmates while looking into the eyes of another, "should you listen to her and not ride that horse the same day?"

She didn't wait for an answer. "No! Because I may like someone, who likes a friend of mine, who introduces us both to someone else who doesn't like either of us—*who cares?*" She flung up her arms. "Let's move on!" Keeping her arms raised, she strode like a supermodel down the middle of the stables. I glanced around for someone to giggle with, but saw only bored twenty-somethings shifting uncomfortably. I guess this wasn't going to turn out to be one of those unexpected romance stories for *Mademoiselle* after all.

Our last stop was a fenced arena where two women showed us the different styles of riding. When one of the horses spooked, and the rider couldn't control him, confusion and alarm spread through our little group. In an instant, the horses veered from sweetly vulnerable to sneaky and dangerous.

"I'm *really* glad that happened," Roberta announced when the horse finally calmed down. We could see that mistakes happen, she said. It was all part of what she called the "human factor." It was already worth the $150 just to see Roberta as a glass-half-full-type of person.

As I headed back to my car that night, I contemplated asking at the registration desk if I could trade in my remaining lessons for a chance to follow Roberta around. She was the most fun I'd had since I'd heard the words, "I don't think we should see each other any more," and I was hungry for more.

The next week I was introduced to my horse, who was billed as one of the "oldest and sweetest" they had. You had me at oldest, I thought, already feeling a kinship. Nevada was a soft brown with long eyelashes that lined big, dark pools of gentleness. We looked each other over.

"It's a little chilly out here now," I said, and smiled awkwardly. Nevada gave me a quick look and then turned his head to stare off into the distance. *Great*, I thought, *I didn't come here to be judged and rejected again.* I reached out a hand to stroke his back anyway, and his coat felt warm under my palm. It gave me an idea. It was getting cold out—maybe he could help.

As I leaned into Nevada's side, I was startled when it felt like he leaned back. As his warmth spread up my shoulder, I turned to flatten my upper body against his. He shifted his feet and snorted, but continued to press into me, and within seconds my body temperature had reached a comfortable level again. I kissed the flat, coarse hairs of his shoulder, and hugged him around the part of his neck that I could reach. "You're the nicest horse ever," I told him, relieved.

Roberta led us single file into the riding area, and we lined up a safe distance from each other. Told that we would mount "in a timely fashion," there was no time for mental preparation before Roberta hoisted me up and over. "Grab his hair or his saddle, girl, or we'll be scraping you out of the dirt when you land on the other side!"

I couldn't stand the idea of pulling Nevada's hair after what we'd just experienced together, but the saddle horn was not a satisfactory anchor either.

"Look, we're losing her," announced Roberta as I felt myself sliding off. But then Nevada shifted his weight and rolled me gently the other way. He lifted and dropped his hooves slowly, and after a minute I got used to the shifts in gravity and relaxed against him.

"Now listen up! These old horses don't want to move unless they have to. I want you to kick them—*lightly* people!—and get them moving. I'm gonna teach you how to ride what's called the posting trot."

She climbed on a horse and urged him into a slow jog, counting, "One-two, one-two, you see how that's matching my horse's movements? One-two, one-two. Now you count out loud with me. I CAN'T HEAR YOU PEOPLE!" Afraid of some kind of horsey court martial, we all began mumbling, "One-two, one-two."

Roberta then began to stand and sit in her saddle, and we each took a crack at it. It's a fabulous thing once you get the rhythm of it—a completely painless way to ride. I didn't get the hang of it that night, but I was guffawing so hard by the end of the lesson that I couldn't even get the "one-two, one-two" out anymore. *Boyfriend, shmoyfriend,* I thought on the drive home. *When did I ever laugh that hard with him?*

On our final night together, I thanked Nevada for being so nice to me, "I mean, for not killing me and stuff." As I waited for my class to start, a man I hadn't seen before walked towards me out of the darkness.

"Hi there!" he called. "How's it going?"

I smiled politely, "Fine, thanks."

"You going to the hayride next weekend?"

I had a vague memory of a flyer about an upcoming event with horses, wagons, and a potluck "family style" barbecue, which I took to mean a rodeo of dysfunction garnished with crappy food.

"I'm afraid I won't be able t—"

"Good horsie, huh, goooood horsie," the man suddenly slapped two meaty hands onto Nevada's forehead. I gaped as he dragged them slowly down Nevada's velvety nose. The horse flattened his ears.

"Hey, Bob, you need to finish cleaning your horse!" a woman yelled from the stalls. I smiled with relief as he jogged back to the stables.

"What the hell was that?" I said to the night air, and the usually sedate Nevada swung his head around to look right at me, rolling his eyes in commiseration. It was such a human gesture that it caught me even more off guard than Bob-the-horse-groper's sleazy come-on. "I *know*, right?" I laughed. "I thought it was just *me*!" I smoothed the ruffled hairs on his forehead.

I finally learned the posting trot that night, or rather, Nevada learned to time his gait to my predictably off-kilter movements. It felt like a sweet way to end our short yet meaningful relationship. I made a mental note to thank the friend who'd talked me into leaving my house in the first place.

I still had a way to go before I felt ready to hop back into the dating saddle again, but I knew something I hadn't known back when I'd been nursing the impotent fury of rejection in my apartment. Being alone is not an inherently painful state; it was being alone with too much time to think about why I'd been dumped that had truly stung me. In a way, the writers of those *Cosmo* articles were onto something, but not in the way they thought. Going out on solo adventures had turned out to be a way to court myself, not to impress strange men so I wouldn't have to be alone. As it turned out, I hadn't been lonely for my ex-boyfriend, but in need of a self-image that didn't include terms like "dump-able." Who would have thought that the friendship of an old nag could have convinced me, finally, that I wasn't one myself?

—JOAN KELLY

A Perfect Moment

The Western saddle felt light in my arms as I settled it on the rack and lay the sweat-soaked saddle pad on top. I walked out of the barn, into the morning sun and over to Ginger, who was tied to one of three giant tractor tires, each three-and-a-half feet tall, the centers filled with hay. Ginger swung her head to watch me, nostrils blowing puffs of steam, and she lowered her face until it was eye level with mine. I slipped her bridle off, looping it over my shoulder. I was fourteen, and I'd never been happier.

Ginger was, appropriately, a gingerbread-colored mare, nondescript, average height, and a quarter horse through and through. I'd swear that she could smell a cow from fifty miles. I had been to this 20,000-acre Central California cattle ranch twice before in the summers, for a two-week horse camp—the pinnacle of my existence, and something I financed with money I had saved all year long. This year, I was invited to spring roundup, seven days over spring break from my freshman year in high school—half the state and a world away. This was a chance to be a real cowgirl and help bring in the new calves. Becka and Suzanne, two other summer camp girlfriends of mine, were also invited, and we spent our nights in a warm bedroom in the owners' house rather than the bunkhouse outside.

Papa Bear and Mama Bear, as the owners liked to be called, picked me up from the Greyhound bus depot on a cold Saturday evening. I would meet my mount at the crack of dawn. The Bears were graying ranchers with a calf-roping daughter and five-year-old granddaughter. Papa Bear was a short, squat man, craggy-faced, leathery-skinned, and bow-legged. He wore old blue jeans and classic cowboy boots and always walked as if he'd just spent twelve hours in the saddle. Not the Marlboro man, but a real, no-nonsense cowpoke. Mama Bear, even shorter than her husband, was a gruff, tough woman with sparkling blue eyes and wild white hair. Not as easygoing as Papa Bear, she was slow to trust a child, but once you won her over, she was your friend for life.

Ginger had been purchased at auction the year before. She was already saddled and tied to the hitching tires that day, and Mama Bear explained that Ginger always wore her halter—even under her bridle—because she had been abused and was "head shy." Ginger was afraid of being hit and it was difficult to put anything on her head or over her ears, let alone touch her there, she said. "Papa Bear is the only one who can put her bridle on or take it off," she told me.

I had just begun to stroke Ginger on the shoulder, by way of introduction, when Papa Bear strode up with her bridle. Ginger tossed her head high and stamped her feet, rearing and straining against her lead rope, her eyes large and white. The cowboy gripped the horse by her lip and forced the bridle on and back over her ears. When he released her, she was a shaking, terrified mess, and when I reached out to pat her side, she flinched and backed away.

I stared at this wild-eyed horse, a little afraid for myself. I felt Becka at my side. "You don't have to do it like that," she said quietly. I wasn't supposed to bridle her at all, I thought.

"She's a good horse, with a lot of cow sense," Mama Bear reassured me. And I placed the sharp toe of my cowboy boot in the stirrup and swung into the saddle.

We rode at a walk far out into the hills that morning, the girls, the Bears, and I, with a handful of serious cowboys rounding out our group. Ginger kept her head down, all business and slightly bored, I thought. When we finally came upon a large, grazing herd of cattle in the distance, Ginger came alive beneath me. I felt her energy surge as she picked up her pace, holding her head aloft, ears erect and trained forward, eyes riveted on the animals ahead.

The cattle drive, something I had dreamed of doing since watching Wild West roundups on reruns of *The Big Valley* and *Bonanza*, was slower and more deliberate than I had imagined. But my adrenalin did not wane. The cowboys told us to fan out and keep our distance from the wary herd, which began to move in the right direction as soon as we were a hundred yards away. We were told to stay quiet and not scare them. Then we slowly escorted them down toward the ranch.

I watched the cowboys dash off on occasion to turn the strays that inevitably spooked, and I silently wished for a cow to bolt on me. Then it happened. A shaggy brown heifer took off to the right just ahead. Ginger needed no instruction. Before I could begin to turn her, she arced outside of the cow's path and steered it back to the herd. Mama Bear smiled. I felt a surge of joy. I patted Ginger on the neck. "Thank you," I whispered to her. An ear flicked back toward me, then forward again.

We picked up smaller groups of cattle all the way down and arrived at the ranch that evening. After a hearty dinner and a full night's sleep, we awoke to the predawn sounds of Papa Bear yipping and yelling on the hillsides as he single-handedly brought in the animals that had strayed during the night. The girls and I wouldn't do any working riding that day; we would just hang out with our horses and watch the cowboys brand and castrate the calves. Papa Bear had bridled Ginger by grabbing her lip again, and I was determined to end her torture.

I stood with Ginger, who was tied to the fence. Calf after bawling calf was pinned, branded, and castrated. Though I was not as distressed over this scene then as I would be now, after several minutes I had watched enough and I turned my attention to Ginger. I stroked her neck and whispered loving nonsense to her. I let my fingers travel up her neck, only until she flinched, and then I lowered them down and started again. I took a hoof pick and cleaned her hooves. I brushed her, again working my way up her neck and down again. I fed her carrots and sweet grass. We rode around the grounds and practiced roping fence posts. I adored her all day long.

I left for the barn a little early that evening and tied Ginger to the tire. We were alone. She immediately tossed her head high above me. "Well, girl," I told her, "You can trust me. I will never, ever hurt you." I stroked her neck as I had done before, slowly working my way up. She snorted and threw her head way back. If I stood on tiptoe, I thought, I might just reach her ear. I could hear the sounds of Papa Bear and the others, talking, joking, winding their way up toward the barn from down below. I tickled Ginger's cheek, whispering to her, making sweet shushing sounds. Quickly, I stretched my hand up to her ear and flicked the bridle over. Ginger startled, shook her head, and I reached over and flipped the other side off.

I walked to the tack room with the bridle over my shoulder, saddle in my arms, just as Papa Bear rode up. He saw me and nodded.

We spent a week riding with Mama Bear, collecting cows, and hanging out with the horses. Every day, I would put Ginger's bridle on in the morning and take it off in the afternoon in the same manner, tickling her neck, her cheek, and then flipping the leather strap over her ear. Each day, it got easier. By Friday, two days before I would leave the ranch, Ginger would lower her head so I could reach her easily, and I no longer had to play the tickling game.

Our last morning together, Mama Bear told me and my friends that we could go riding together, unsupervised by grownups, on the flats by the river. I would finally get my high-speed Wild West ride. I'll never forget that golden morning, the wet, shiny grass, the sunlight glinting off the water, the full-throttle galloping race across the sandy bottom, all of us yelling and whooping and red faced, the horses prancing and spirited and free.

Back to the barn we girls rode, feeling both elated and melancholy. I would ride the Greyhound at noon.

For those of us fortunate enough to have experienced them, there are perfect moments, when time seems to stand still, and the earth stops spinning and everything goes quiet, moments of absolute bliss. As adults, we can draw upon these moments in times of stress and trouble, and it quiets and centers and grounds us.

I climbed up and sat on the tire, legs dangling, facing Ginger. She stepped forward, closing the gap between us, and pressed the length of her head into my chest and belly. I wrapped my arms around her, nestling my cheek against her forehead and closing my eyes. The world went still. I have no idea how long we sat there. I remember my friends, respectful and silent. I remember hearing the bell clanging for us to come down to breakfast. I remember the sun, warm on my eyelids.

—INDI ZELENY

Contributors

SUE PEARSON ATKINSON ("Max the Magnificent") has worked for thirty years as a broadcast journalist and is currently an independent producer of nationally distributed public television programs. She and her neurologist husband, Rick, raised five children and taught them all to ride, but none of them developed her passion for all things equine. She's hoping her granddaughter will someday share her obsession.

WENDY BETH BAKER ("Something about Mollie") lives in Los Angeles, where she is an editor at Yahoo. She is the author of *Healing Power of Horses: Lessons from the Lakota Indians.*

DEBORAH K. BUNDY ("The Flint Hills") lives in Columbus, North Carolina, with her husband, three horses, three dogs, and one barn cat. Her work has been published in the *Kansas City Star*, *Kentucky Derby Magazine*, *Horse Canada*, and *Chronicle of the Horse*, and anthologies by Whispering Prairie Press and Potpourri Publishing. Her writing has won awards from *ByLine Magazine*, the Ozarks Writers Conference, and the Oklahoma Writers Conference.

CANDACE CARRABUS ("Deby Delivers") has been riding horses and writing stories—frequently simultaneously—for a long time. She infuses her writing with the mystery and spirituality horses bring to her life. She keeps three horses on a farm outside St. Louis, Missouri, where she lives with her husband and daughter. You can visit her Web site at *www.candacecarrabus.com.*

Paula Corbett ("Only the Best") is a sometime-ESL teacher, sometime-freelance writer, and constant student of life, who divides her time between British Columbia, Asia, and points yet unknown. She loves the smell of horses and enjoys all kinds of sports for all the right reasons.

Jill Cordover ("The Horse of My Dreams") is a freelance writer who lives in a small motor home that she parks in San Luis Obispo, California, when she isn't traveling the country looking for adventure. She is one link in a long line of horse-crazy women. She has pictures of her grandmother jumping sidesaddle, and her daughter trains event horses.

Charlotte Davidson ("My Old Man") was born and raised in Southern California. After college, she spent eleven years in Paris. She holds a master's degree in English from Syracuse University and an M.F.A. in poetry from the University of California-Irvine. She now lives part-time in Los Angeles and part-time in Riverside, where she teaches college English and takes care of her six cats, four dogs, three horses, and one husband. Her two children live in Europe.

Gail Folkins ("From Horseback") is a graduate student in creative writing at Texas Tech University. She writes creative nonfiction and poetry. Her recent works include the essay, "Dance Hall Revival," winner of the 2004 Lawrence Clayton Award from the Southwest Popular Culture and American Culture

Association. When she's not writing or teaching, she enjoys horseback riding and travel.

Kimberley Freeman ("Galloping into Forty") is a professional freelance copywriter (*www.zagstudios.com*) and a part-time English tutor in Atlanta. She has won prizes for her short fiction, and her work has appeared in *Literally Horses, Insolent Rudder, Cenotaph, Horse Miracles* (Adams Media), and an anthology of the South's *Newest and Most Promising Writers.* She serves as vice-president of the Georgia Authors Guild and is a member of Georgia Writers and the Equine Rescue League. When the advertising world gets frustrating, she enjoys galloping across fields on her horse, Red Rabbit.

Joanne M. Friedman ("Left in the Lust") has spent more than forty years around horses. She owns and operates Gallant Hope Farm in northwest New Jersey. A veteran English teacher and freelance writer, she is the author of *It's a Horse's Life! Advice and Observations for the Humans Who Choose to Share It.*

Kay George ("Merlin") is retired and lives with a dog and a cat in the San Francisco Bay Area, where she settled with her husband over forty years ago. She grew up and attended college in Pennsylvania and worked for many years transcribing and editing technical publications for a translation agency. She has four grown children.

Star Hughes ("Just Bless") began her equestrian career in Tennessee, riding and showing American Saddlebreds, hunters, and quarter horses. She later achieved Horsemaster status in combined training at the Potomac Horse Center. She holds certifications in areas ranging from dressage to therapeutic riding and vaulting. Now, with over thirty years' experience in training horses and riders, she has created the Centaur Seat method of riding. In her business, EquesTraining, she uses the proven techniques of Linda Tellington-Jones, known as "the Touch that Teaches," to improve communication between horses and humans.

SUSAN HUTCHINSON ("Experiencing Murphy") has lived most of her life in Seattle, Washington. She earned a degree in business management and worked in the finance industry until she took early retirement in 2003. She enjoys writing poetry and spending time outdoors, particularly horseback riding and playing with her dog, Cinder.

SANDY JENSEN ("Home after Dark") is a native of Wenatchee, Washington, who now lives in Eugene, Oregon. She is a three-time Teacher-of-the-Year who specializes in teaching fiction, poetry, and other forms of writing and literature at the community college level. She has published short stories, essays, and poetry for thirty years. After civilizing four unruly children, Lance, the horse in the story, retired to a long and happy life in the green pastures of the Skagit Valley.

JOAN KELLY ("Going Solo") lives in Los Angeles and is crazy about all animals. Her work has been featured in such publications as *Ben Is Dead* and *Kitchen Sink Magazine,* and she is currently working on a nonfiction book project. Despite the posting trot, she prefers petting and hugging horses to riding them.

Loretta Kemsley ("The Biggest Step") grew up in the San Fernando Valley when it was dominated by ranches and movie stables. Surrounded by trainers of extraordinary skill, she moved naturally into the world of horse shows and rodeos. After twenty years as a public trainer, she turned to private equestrian pursuits. Her memories of the great horses that have graced her life have appeared in several books, including *The Encyclopedia of TV Pets* and *A Cup of Comfort for Courage*. You can reach her at *lkemsley@moondance.org.*

Lucy S. Lauer ("A Horse Named Kat") grew up in Houston, Texas, and now lives with her husband, Michael, in Leawood, Kansas. They have two grown children. She is a professional counselor in private practice and has published a children's health and fitness cookbook, poetry, short fiction, and numerous articles in *Kansas City Parent* and other news magazines.

Meera Lester ("Horseplay") grew up around horses on a farm in Boone County, Missouri. When she was twenty-two, she changed her name from Betsy Lou. She now lives in San Jose, California, where she writes mainly nonfiction books. Her newest is *Mary Magdalene: The Modern Guide to the Bible's Most Mysterious and Misunderstood Woman*. Once a month, she rides horses along the Pacific Ocean.

Jacklyn Lee Lindstrom ("The Horse Nobody Wanted") has been a horse lover since day one. For twenty years she and her family raised and showed horses from their small farm in Minnesota. Now retired and living in Spearfish, South Dakota, she finds the stirrups too high and the ground too hard, so she lives her passion for horses through painting and writing.

Reba Ellen Logan ("Thunder Rescued Me") has worked in human services for over twenty-five years. She is a licensed professional counselor currently working at a private psychiatric hospital in Chattanooga, Tennessee, where she specializes in helping victims of trauma, abuse, domestic violence, eating disorders, and mood disorders. She lives on a small farm with her husband, Bobby, a cat, a Sheltie, two horses, and a family of crows. Her two grown children, Misty and Daniel, are also pursuing careers in psychiatric fields.

Stephanie Losee ("It's Only a Paper Horse") is a former writer for *Fortune* whose work has also appeared in the *Los Angeles Times*, the *New York Post*, *Family Money*, the *Mountain Gazette*, and *Child*. An excerpt from her memoir-in-progress was a finalist for the New Letters Award in creative nonfiction. She lives in San Francisco with her husband and three daughters.

Charlotte Mendel ("Mucho Muchacho") lives in Nova Scotia where she works as an instructional designer. She has published articles in *City Lights*, the Tel Aviv supplement of *The Jerusalem Post*, and *The Bluenose Tribune*. Her fiction has appeared in *The*

Nashwaak Review and *The Shore Magazine*. She has two young children and has been heard to mutter, "I should have stuck with horses." Poteet lived to the ripe old age of thirty-one, but Muchacho inexplicably died at fourteen.

Paula Munier ("If Wishes Were Horses") has worked in publishing as a writer and editor for nearly twenty years. The mother of three lives in southern Massachusetts with her family, two dogs, and a cat. She plans to add "dapple gray mare" to that list soon.

Marcia Rudoff ("We Are Not Afraid of the Horse") lives in Bainbridge Island, Washington. She is a freelance writer and memoir writing teacher whose published works have appeared in *Northwest Runner*, *Seattle Times*, *Stories with Grace*, *A Cup of Comfort for Inspiration*, and the *Bainbridge Island Review*, for which she writes the monthly column, "Senior Outlook." Her other interests include her children, grandchildren, baseball, and chocolate.

Kay Sexton ("*Vieux Chapeau* (Old Hat)") divides her time between England, the United States, and the South of France. She is a philosophy graduate, recreational runner, and hostage to a capricious muse. Her Web site *www.charybdis.co.uk* contains her current and forthcoming publications.

Ariana Strozzi ("Sandy Hears the Call") holds a degree in zoology and is an internationally respected pioneer and teacher of Equine Guided Education. She has been working with horses since 1970 and bringing the magic of horse communication to people from all walks of life since 1990 at Strozzi Ranch in California (*www.strozziranch.com*). Ariana has won championship awards in dressage, eventing, jumping, reining, and working cowhorse. Her latest book is *Horse Sense for the Leader Within.*

HILARY C. T. WALKER ("The Gift Horse") is a British citizen, but hopes that won't be held against her. She lives in Richmond, Virginia, with her husband, son, four horses, three dogs, and three cats. Hilary's award-winning short stories can be found in her book, *Pithy Pieces by a Palmy Penman.* Her last fall off a horse was from Kinley, an expensive eventer, into a ditch at a one-day event in South Carolina. If she'd been riding Kelly, it never would have happened.

SAMANTHA DUCLOUX WALTZ ("Slender Threads") has published fiction and nonfiction under the names Samellyn Wood, Samantha Ducloux, and Samantha Ducloux Waltz. Her current passion is making sense out of her world by writing personal essays. She lives in Portland, Oregon, with her husband, a very large dog, and a very small cat. Her mare Vida lives nearby and gives her many quiet hours of pleasure in the arena and on the trail.

IRENE WANNER ("Terrible Trina") teaches fiction writing at Seattle's Richard Hugo House and the University of Washington Women's Center, and reviews books for several periodicals, including the *Los Angeles Times*, *Orion*, and *Bird Watcher's Digest.* She is a member of the Northwest Independent Editors Guild. Her story collection, *Sailing to Corinth*, won the 1988 Western States Arts Federation award for fiction. She spends autumns in Jemez Springs,

New Mexico, where she is working on a book of natural history essays.

CAROLE WATERHOUSE ("Raising Tagel") is a creative writing professor at California University of Pennsylvania and the author of a novel, *Without Wings*, and a short story collection, *The Paradise Ranch*. She lives on a ten-acre farm in western Pennsylvania with her husband and three horses.

CHERYL E. WILLIAMS ("Never Too Young, Never Too Old") cherishes her childhood memories of the time she spent on her grandparents' farm near Uniontown, Pennsylvania. A Penn State graduate, she now lives in the Pittsburgh area where creative writing, volunteer work, and family activities fill her time.

INDI ZELENY ("A Perfect Moment") is a California writer and editor. She lives in the country with her husband, mother, two small children, two dogs, and two cats. She loves warm summer evenings, Third World travel, and a really good cup of Mexican hot chocolate. She is the editor of a women's anthology titled *HerStory: What I Learned in My Bathtub ... and More True Stories on Life, Love, and Other Inconveniences* which was released in October 2005 by Adams Media; and she is writing two young-adult novels.

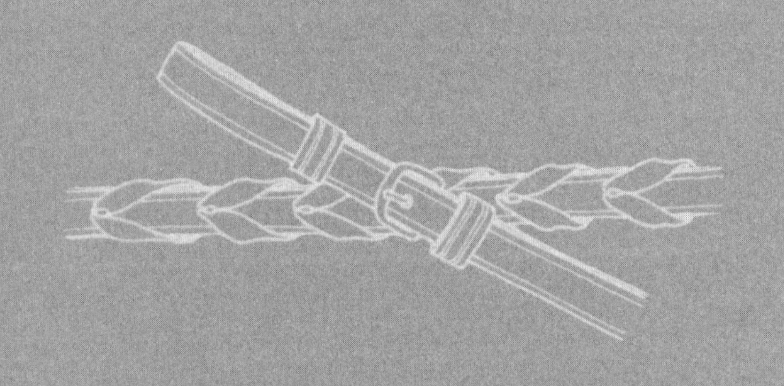

About the Editor

A. Bronwyn Llewellyn has enjoyed a long career in the museum profession, researching, writing, and editing dozens of exhibits on such diverse topics as high technology, garbage, regional history, the civil rights movement, honeybees, the Vietnam War, and ancient Chinese astronomy. She holds a bachelor's degree in English from William Jewell College in Missouri and a master's in museum studies from the Cooperstown Graduate Program in Upstate New York. Her books include *The Goddess at Home: Divine Interiors Inspired by Aphrodite, Artemis, Athena, Demeter, Hera, Hestia, and Persephone* (Rockport); *The Goddess Home Style Guide* (Rockport); *The Shakespeare Oracle* (Fair Winds Press); and *Blooming Rooms: Decorating with Flowers and Floral Motifs*, with Meera Lester (Rockport). Her essay, "The Gift of Horses," won first prize in the 2004 essay contest sponsored by 84 Charing Cross Bookstore in Cleveland, Ohio.

She enjoys knitting, making handmade books and jewelry, and writing fiction and screenplays. And she is still horse crazy, after all these years. Her horse-deprived childhood only stoked her passion. Now she indulges it by volunteering at a therapeutic riding center. You can see Odie, Harley, Six, Ben, and all the other wonderful horses—and people—there by visiting *www.nceft.org.*